THE ULTIMATE
Low Fat Baking
COOKBOOK

THE ULTIMATE
Low Fat Baking
COOKBOOK

The best-ever step-by-step collection of low-fat baking recipes for
tempting and healthy eating

Consultant Editor: Linda Fraser

INDEX

This edition first published in 1998 by Lorenz Books

© Anness Publishing Limited 1998

Lorenz Books is an imprint of
Anness Publishing Limited
Hermes House
88–89 Blackfriars Road
London SE1 8HA

This edition published in 1998 for Index

ISBN 1 85967 693 6

A CIP catalogue record for this book is available
from the British Library

Publisher: Joanna Lorenz
Senior Editor: Cathy Marriott
Designer: Lilian Lindblom
Illustrations: Anna Koska

COOK'S NOTE
For all recipes, quantities are given in both metric
and imperial measures and, where appropriate,
measures are also given in standard cups and
spoons. Follow one set, but not a mixture, because
they are not interchangeable.

Printed and bound in Germany

10 9 8 7 6 5 4 3 2 1

Contents

Introduction

When we talk of cakes and baking we tend to imagine rich, calorie-laden treats that are well out of reach if you are following a low fat diet. With reduced-fat cooking methods, however, it is very easy to create delicious, low fat desserts, cakes and bakes that are also full of flavour and appeal. It is generally agreed that a high fat diet is bad for us, especially if the fats are of the saturated variety. Unless you are making meringues or angel cakes, it is rarely possible to do entirely without fat in baking. Nevertheless, it is possible to cut down considerably on the amount used, and equally good results can be achieved using unsaturated oils instead of saturated fats.

Polyunsaturated oils such as sunflower oil, corn oil and safflower oil are excellent for most baking purposes, but choose olive oil which is mono-unsaturated for recipes that require a good, strong flavour. When an oil is not suitable, a soft margarine which is high in polyunsaturates is the fat to choose. Low fat spreads are ideal for spreading but not good for baking, as they contain a high proportion of water.

Although cheese is high in saturated fat, its flavour makes it invaluable in many recipes. Choose either reduced-fat or half-fat varieties with a mature flavour, or a lesser amount of a highly flavoured cheese such as Parmesan. When using less fat, you can add extra moisture to cakes and teabreads in the form of fresh or dried fruits. There is no need to use full cream milk – try skimmed milk or fruit juice instead. Buttermilk (the liquid left over from churning butter) is, surprisingly, virtually fat free and is perfect for soda bread and scones. Cream undoubtedly adds a touch of luxury to special occasion cakes, however, fromage frais, thick yogurt or curd cheese sweetened with honey make delicious low fat fillings and toppings for even the most elaborate cakes.

So you will see that using less fat doesn't prevent you from making scrumptious cakes and bakes that look and taste every bit as good as those made traditionally with butter and cream. The recipes in this book are sure to inspire, impress and amaze everyone who believed low fat baking to be an idea too good to be true.

Left: Everyone loves fresh breads, scones and biscuits straight from the oven.

Store Cupboard

Cutting down on fat doesn't mean sacrificing taste. Instead, choose ingredients that are naturally lower in fat. This is not so limiting as it sounds, as the following ingredients show.

flour

FLOURS

Mass-produced, highly refined flours are fine for most baking purposes, but for the very best results choose organic stone-ground flours because they will add flavour as well as texture to your baking.

Rye flour

This dark-coloured flour has a low gluten content and gives a dense loaf with a good flavour. It is best mixed with strong wheat flour to give a lighter loaf.

Soft flour

This flour, sometimes called sponge flour, contains less gluten than plain flour and is ideal for light cakes and biscuits.

Strong flour

Made from hard wheat which contains a high proportion of gluten, this flour is the one to use for bread-making.

Wholemeal flour

Because this flour contains the complete wheat kernel, it gives a coarser texture and a good wholesome flavour to bread.

NUTS AND SEEDS

Most nuts are low in saturated fats and high in polyunsaturated fats. Use them sparingly as their total fat content is high. Sunflower seeds, poppy and linseeds are good for decorating rolls or adding texture.

YEAST

Dried yeast helps bread to rise.

HERBS AND SPICES

Chopped fresh herbs add a great deal of interest to baking. They add flavour to breads, scones and soda breads. In the absence of fresh herbs, dried herbs can be used: less is needed but the flavour is generally not as good.

Spices can add either strong or subtle flavours depending on the amount used. Ground cinnamon, nutmeg and mixed spice are most useful for baking but more exotic spices, such as saffron or cardamom, can also be used to great effect.

Buy herbs and spices from a shop with a high turnover to ensure optimum freshness and flavour.

bottled apricots

SWEETENERS

Dried fruits

These are a traditional addition to cakes and teabreads. There is a wide range available, including more unusual varieties such as peach, pineapple, banana and mango, as well as more familiar currants and glacé cherries. Natural sugars in dried fruits add sweetness to baked goods and keep them moist, making it possible to use less fat.

Fruit juice

Concentrated fruit juices are very useful for baking. They have no added sweeteners or preservatives and can be diluted as required. Use them in their concentrated form for baking or for sweetening fillings.

dried pineapple

Honey

Good honey has a strong flavour so you can use rather less of it than the equivalent amount of sugar. It also contains traces of minerals and vitamins.

Malt extract

This is a sugary by-product of barley. It has a strong flavour and is ideal for bread, cakes and teabreads as it adds moisture.

dried yeast

Molasses

This is the residue left after the first stage of refining sugar cane. It has a strong, smoky and slightly bitter taste that gives a good flavour to bakes and cakes. Black treacle can often be used as a substitute for molasses.

Pear and apple spread

This is a very concentrated fruit juice with no added sugar. It has a sweet-sour taste and can be used as a spread or blended with a little fruit juice and added to baking recipes as a sweetener.

Unrefined sugars

Most baking recipes call for sugar; choose unrefined sugar rather than refined sugars, as they have more flavour and contain some minerals.

Right: It's easier to follow a healthy eating plan if you have a store cupboard full of tempting ingredients that are naturally low in fat.

light muscovado sugar

currants   *poppy seeds*   *honey*   *herbs*

it   *oatmeal*   *cinnamon sticks*   *dried apricots*   *sesame s*

sunflower seeds

physalis

linseed

ns   *glacé cherries*   *olive oil*   *pear and apple spread*   *apricot compôte*   *dates*

extra virgin olive oil

fresh fruit

orange juice

blueberries

Oils, Fats and Dairy Produce

LOW FAT OILS AND FATS

Low fat spreads are ideal for spreading on breads and teabreads, but are unfortunately not suitable for baking because they have a high water content.

When you are baking, try to avoid saturated fats such as butter and hard margarine and use oils high in polyunsaturates such as sunflower, corn or safflower oil. When margarine is essential, choose a variety that is high in polyunsaturates.

Low fat spread, rich buttermilk blend

Made with a high proportion of buttermilk, which is naturally low in fat. Unsuitable for baking.

Olive oil

Use this mono-unsaturated oil when a recipe requires a good strong flavour. It is best to use extra virgin olive oil.

Olive oil reduced-fat spread

Based on olive oil, this spread has a better flavour that some other low fat spreads, but is not suitable for baking.

Reduced-fat butter

This contains about 40% fat; the rest is water and milk solids emulsified together. It is not suitable for baking.

Sunflower light

Not suitable for baking as it contains only 40% fat, plus emulsified water and milk solids.

Sunflower oil

High in polyunsaturates, this is the oil used most frequently in this book as it has a pleasant but not too dominant flavour.

Very low fat spread

Contains only 20–30% fat and so is not suitable for baking.

LOW FAT CHEESES

There are a lot of low fat cheeses that can be used in baking. Generally, harder cheeses have a higher fat content than soft cheeses. Choose mature cheese whenever possible as you need less of it to give a good flavour.

Cottage cheese

A low fat soft cheese that is also available in a half-fat form.

Curd cheese

This is a low fat soft cheese made with either skimmed or semi-skimmed milk and can be used instead of cheese.

Edam and Maasdam

Two medium fat hard cheeses well suited to baking.

Feta cheese

This is a medium-fat cheese with a firm, crumbly texture. It has a slightly sour, salty flavour which can range from rather bland to strong.

Half-fat Cheddar and Red Leicester

These contain about 14% fat.

Mozzarella light

This is a medium fat version of an Italian soft cheese.

Quark

Made from fermented skimmed milk, this soft, white cheese is virtually free of fat.

CREAM ALTERNATIVES

Yogurt and fromage frais make excellent alternatives to cream, and when combined with honey, liqueurs or other flavourings they make delicious fillings or toppings for cakes and bakes.

Bio yogurt

This contains friendly bacterial cultures that aid digestion. Bio yogurt has a mild, sweet taste.

Crème fraîche

This thick soured cream has a mild, lemony taste. Look out for half-fat créme fraîche which has a fat content of 15%.

Fromage frais

This is a fresh soft cheese available in two grades: virtually fat free (0.4% fat), and a more creamy variety (7.9% fat).

Greek yogurt

This thick, creamy yogurt is made from whole milk with a fat content of 10%. A low fat version is also available.

Left: Try to avoid using saturated fats such as butter and margarine. Instead use oils or spreads high in polyunsaturates.

curd cheese

cottage cheese

Edam

Mozzarella

Maasdam

Cheddar

feta

Red Leicester

soft cheese

quark

semi-skimmed milk

buttermilk

low fat yogurt

half-fat crème fraîche

eggs

bio yogurt

light fromage frais

Above: There are a whole range of low fat cheeses that can be used in baking.

Left: Use low fat milks for baking and try yogurt or fromage frais as an alternative to cream.

LOW FAT MILKS

Buttermilk

Made from skimmed milk with a bacterial culture added, it is very low in fat.

Powdered skimmed milk

A useful, low fat standby.

Semi-skimmed milk

With a fat content of only 1.5–1.8%, this milk tastes less rich than full-cream milk. It is favoured by many people for everyday use for precisely this reason.

Skimmed milk

This milk has had virtually all fat removed leaving 0.1–0.3%. It is ideal for those wishing to cut down their fat intake.

EGGS

These are essential for baking.

Equipment

If you choose good-quality, heavy-based non-stick cookware, the amount of fat used in baking can be kept to an absolute minimum.

Baking sheet
Choose a large, heavy baking sheet that will not warp at high temperatures.

Balloon whisk
Perfect for whisking egg whites and incorporating air into other light mixtures.

Box grater
This multi-purpose grater can be used for citrus rind, fruit and vegetables, and cheese.

Brown paper
Used for wrapping around the outside of cake tins to protect the cake mixture from the full heat of the oven.

Cake tester
A simple implement that, when inserted into a cooked cake, will come out clean if the cake is ready.

Cook's knife
This has a heavy, wide blade and is ideal for chopping.

Deep round cake tin
This deep tin is ideal for baking fruit cakes.

Electric whisk
Ideal for creaming cake mixtures, whipping cream and whisking egg whites.

Honey twirl
For spooning honey without making a mess!

Juicer
Made from porcelain, glass or plastic – used for squeezing the juice from citrus fruits.

Loaf tin
Available in various sizes and used for making loaf-shaped breads and teabreads.

Measuring jug
Absolutely essential for measuring any kind of liquid accurately.

Measuring spoons
Standard measuring spoons are essential for measuring small quantities of ingredients.

Mixing bowls
A set of different sized bowls is essential in any kitchen for whisking and mixing.

Muffin tin
Shaped into individual cups, this tin is much simpler to use than individual paper cases. It can also be used for baking small pies and tarts.

Non-stick baking paper
For lining tins and baking sheets to ensure cakes, meringues and biscuits do not stick.

Nutmeg grater
This miniature grater is used for grating whole nutmegs.

Nylon sieve
Suitable for most baking purposes, and particularly for sieving foods that react adversely with metal.

Palette knife
This implement is needed for loosening pies, tarts and breads from baking sheets and for smoothing icing over cakes.

Pastry brush
Useful for brushing excess flour from pastry and brushing glazes over pastries, breads and tarts.

Pastry cutters
A variety of shapes and sizes of cutter are useful when stamping out pastry, biscuits and scones.

Rectangular cake tin
For making tray cakes and bakes, served cut into slices.

Ring mould
Perfect for making angel cakes and other ring-shaped cakes.

Sandwich cake tin
Ideal for sponge cakes; make sure you have two of them!

Scissors
Vital for cutting paper and snipping dough and pastry.

Square cake tin
Used for making square cakes or cakes served cut into smaller squares.

Swiss roll tin
This shallow tin is designed especially for Swiss rolls.

Vegetable knife
A useful knife for preparing the fruit and vegetables that you may add to your bakes.

Wire rack
Ideal for cooling cakes and bakes, allowing the circulation of air which will prevent sogginess.

Wire sieve
A large wire sieve is ideal for most normal baking purposes.

Wooden spoon
Essential for mixing ingredients and creaming mixtures.

Right: Invest in a few useful items for easy low fat cooking: non-stick cookware and accurate measuring equipment are essential.

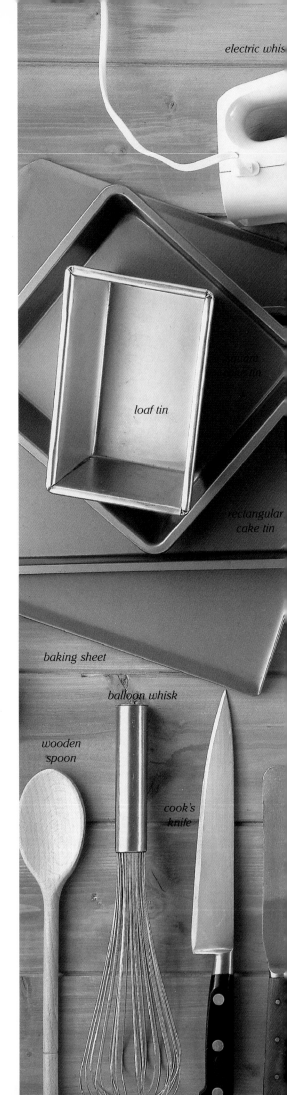

electric whisk

loaf tin

rectangular cake tin

baking sheet

balloon whisk

wooden spoon

cook's knife

mixing bowls

non-stick baking
paper

brown paper

scissors

sandwich
cake tin

ring mould

pastry brush

wire rack

measuring jug

deep round
cake tin

pastry
cutters

ke
ter

egetable knife

honey
whirl

wire rack

ette
vés

Swiss roll tin

juicer

nutmeg
grater

box grater

wire sieve

nylon sieve

measuring
spoons

muffin tin

Facts about Fat

It's easy to cut down on obvious sources of fat such as butter, margarine, cream, whole milk and high fat cheeses, but watch out for "hidden" fats.

Most of us eat more fat every day than the 10g/¼oz that our bodies need; on average we each consume about 115g/4oz fat each day. Current nutritional advice isn't quite that strict on fat intake though, and it suggests that we should limit our daily intake to no more than 30% of total calories. In real terms, this means that for an average intake of 2,000 calories a day, 30% of energy would come from about 600 calories. Since each gram of fat provides 9 calories, your total daily intake should be no more that 67g fat.

Although we may think of cakes and biscuits as sweet foods, more calories come from their fat than from their sugar. Indeed, of the quarter of our fat intake that comes from non-meat sources, a fifth comes from dairy products and margarine and the rest from cakes, biscuits, pastries and other foods. The merits of low fat baking are enormous, as you are able not only to cut down on your fat intake in general, but you also have control over exactly how

much fat you and your family consume on a daily basis and the type of fat it is.

Fats can be divided into two main categories – saturated and unsaturated. We are all well aware of the dangers of saturated fats in relation to blocking arteries and causing coronary heart disease. Much of the saturated fat we eat comes from animal sources – meat and dairy products such as suet, lard and butter – which are solid at room temperature. However, there are also some saturated fats of vegetable origin, notably coconut and palm oils. In addition, a number of margarines are "hydrogenated", a process that increases the proportion of saturated fat they contain. Such margarine should be avoided.

Above: Animal products such as lard, suet, butter and some margarines are major sources of saturated fats.

Left: Some oils, such as olive oil and rapeseed, are thought to help lower blood cholesterol.

The Fat and Calorie Contents of Food

This chart shows the weight of fat and the energy content of 110g/3½oz of various foods.

Unsaturated fats can be divided into two main types: mono-unsaturated and poly-unsaturated. Mono-unsaturated fats are found in various foods including olive oil, rapeseed oil and some nuts. These fats may actually lower blood cholesterol and this could explain why in Mediterranean countries, where olive oil is widely consumed, there is such a low incidence of heart disease.

The most familiar polyunsaturated fats are of vegetable or plant origin and include sunflower oil, corn oil, soya oil, walnut oil and many soft margarines. It was believed at one time that it was beneficial to switch to polyunsaturated fats as they may also help lower cholesterol. Today, however, most experts believe that it is more important to reduce the total intake of all kinds of fat.

Above: Vegetable and plant oils and some margarines are high in polyunsaturated fat.

FRUIT AND NUTS	Fat	Energy
Apples, eating	0.1g	47Kcals/197kJ
Avocados	19.5g	190Kcals/795kJ
Bananas	0.3g	95Kcals/397kJ
Dried mixed fruit	1.6g	227Kcals/950kJ
Grapefruit	0.1g	30Kcals/155kJ
Oranges	0.1g	37Kcals/155kJ
Peaches	0.1g	33Kcals/138kJ
Almonds	55.8g	612Kcals/2560kJ
Brazil nuts	68.2g	682Kcals/2853kJ
Peanut butter, smooth	53.7g	623Kcals/2606kJ
Pine nuts	68.6g	688Kcals/2878kJ

DAIRY PRODUCE, FATS AND OILS	Fat	Energy
Cream, double	48.0g	449Kcals/1897kJ
Cream, single	19.1g	198Kcals/828kJ
Cream, whipping	39.3g	373Kcals/1560kJ
Milk, skimmed	0.1g	33Kcals/130kJ
Milk, whole	3.9g	66Kcals/276kJ
Cheddar cheese	34.4g	412Kcals/1724kJ
Cheddar-type, reduced fat	15.0g	216Kcals/1092kJ
Cream cheese	47.4g	439Kcals/1837kJ
Brie	26.9g	319Kcals/1335kJ
Edam cheese	25.4g	333Kcals/1393kJ
Feta cheese	20.2g	250Kcals/1046kJ
Parmesan cheese	32.7g	452Kcals/1891kJ
Greek yogurt	9.1g	115Kcals/481kJ
Low fat yogurt, natural	0.8g	56Kcals/234kJ
Butter	81.7g	737Kcals/308kJ
Lard	99.0g	891Kcals/3730kJ
Low fat spread	40.5g	390Kcals/1632kJ
Margarine	81.6g	739Kcals/3092kJ
Coconut oil	99.9g	899Kcals/3761kJ
Corn oil	99.9g	899Kcals/3761kJ
Olive oil	99.9g	899Kcals/3761kJ
Safflower oil	99.9g	899Kcals/3761kJ
Eggs (whole)	10.9g	147Kcals/615kJ
Egg white	trace	36Kcals/150kJ
Egg yolk	30.5g	339Kcals/1418kJ

OTHER FOODS	Fat	Energy
Sugar	0	94Kcals/648kJ
Chocolate, milk	30.3g	529Kcals/2213kJ
Honey	0	88Kcals/1205kJ
Jam	0	61Kcals/1092kJ
Marmalade	0	61Kcals/1092kJ
Lemon curd	5.1g	283Kcals/1184kJ

Techniques

Baking is easy and satisfying, even if you're a beginner. Just follow the recipes, the tips and the step-by-step techniques and you will get perfect results every time.

1 For liquids measured in jugs: Use a glass or clear plastic measuring jug. Put the jug on a flat surface and pour in the liquid. Bend down and check that the liquid is exactly level with the marking on the jug, as specified in the recipe.

2 For measuring dry ingredients in a spoon: Fill the spoon with the ingredients. Level the surface even with the brim of the spoon, using the straight edge of a knife.

3 For liquids measured in spoons: Pour the liquid into the measuring spoon, to the brim, and then pour it into the mixing bowl.

FLOUR

4 For measuring flour in a cup or spoon: Scoop the flour from the canister or bag in the measuring cup or spoon. Hold it over the canister or bag and level the surface.

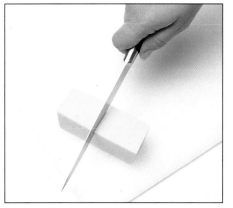

5 For measuring butter: Cut with a sharp knife and weigh, or cut off the specified amount following the markings on the wrapping paper.

6 For rectangular and square cake tins: Measure and cut a strip of grease-proof paper or non-stick baking paper three times as long as the depth of the tin and as wide as the length of the base.

7 For muffin tins: Use paper cases of the required size or grease and flour the tins.

Using Yeast

There are three main types of yeast currently available - dried, easy-blend and fresh. Easy-blend is added directly to the dry ingredients, whereas dried and fresh yeast must first be mixed with warm liquid and a little sugar to activate them.

USING DRIED YEAST

1 Measure dried yeast, then sprinkle it into the warm liquid in a jug or small bowl with a pinch of sugar. Stir well and set aside in a warm place for about 10–15 minutes.

2 When the yeast liquid becomes frothy, stir into the dry ingredients.

Cook's Tip
Dried yeast doesn't dissolve well in milk. You must either leave it for about 30 minutes to froth, or if you are in a hurry, dissolve it in a little water first.

USING EASY-BLEND YEAST

1 Add easy-blend yeast to the dry ingredients directly from the packet. Do not dissolve it in liquid first.

USING FRESH YEAST

1 Place fresh yeast in a small bowl with a pinch of sugar and a little lukewarm water. Cream together until smooth, then leave for 5–10 minutes until frothy, before adding to the dry ingredients.

Making Muffins and Quick Breads

As their name denotes, these bakes are fast and easy to make. The raising agent reacts quickly with moisture and heat to make the muffins and breads rise, without the need for a rising period before baking.

The raising agent is usually bicarbonate of soda or baking powder, which is a mixture of bicarbonate of soda and an acid salt such as cream of tartar. It will start to work as soon as it comes into contact with liquid, so don't mix the dry and liquid ingredients until just before you are ready to fill the muffin tins and bake them.

In addition to the thick-batter quick breads discussed here, there are also quick breads such as scones that are made from soft doughs.

Cook's Tip

Easy-blend (or fast action) is the most readily available dried yeast. Unlike ordinary dried yeast, there is no need to mix it with liquid. Just combine it with the flour and other dry ingredients and then add the warm liquids.

MUFFINS

1 Combine the dry ingredients in a bowl. It is a good idea to sift the flour with the raising agent, salt and any spices to mix them evenly. Add the liquid ingredients and stir just until the dry ingredients are moistened; the mixture will not be smooth. Do not overmix attempting to remove all the lumps. If you do, the muffins will be tough and will have air holes in them.

2 Divide the mixture evenly among the greased muffin tins or deep bun tins lined with paper cases, filling them about two-thirds full. Bake until golden brown and a wooden skewer inserted in the centre comes out clean. To prevent soggy bottoms, remove the muffins immediately from the tins to a wire rack. Cool, and serve warm or at room temperature.

FRUIT AND/OR NUT TEABREADS

1 **Method 1:** Stir together all the liquid ingredients. Add the dry ingredients and beat just until smoothly blended. **Method 2:** Beat the butter with the sugar until the mixture is light and fluffy. Beat in the eggs followed by the other liquid ingredients. Stir in the dry ingredients. Pour the mixture into a prepared tin (typically a loaf tin). Bake until a wooden skewer inserted in the centre comes out clean. If the bread is browning too quickly, cover the top with foil.

2 Cool in the tin for 5 minutes, then turn out on to a wire rack to cool completely. A lengthways crack on the surface is characteristic of teabreads. For easier slicing, wrap the bread in grease-proof paper and overwrap in foil, then store overnight at room temperature.

Making Breadsticks and Focaccia

Italian flatbreads such as focaccia and breadsticks can be topped with herbs and seeds for tasty accompaniments or starters.

Personalize breadsticks and focaccia with combinations of your favourite ingredients for unusual snacks, or split and fill flat-breads with ham or cheese for an Italian-style sandwich. This basic dough can be used for other recipes, such as pizza. The dough may be frozen before it is baked, and thawed before filling.

BREADSTICKS

1 There's no need for the first rising. Divide the dough into walnut-size pieces and roll out on a floured surface with your hands, into thin sausage shapes. Transfer to a greased baking sheet, cover and leave in a warm place for 10–15 minutes. Bake until crisp.

FOCACCIA

1 Warm a mixing bowl by swirling some hot water in it. Drain. Place the yeast in the bowl and pour on the warm water. Stir in the sugar, mix with a fork, and allow to stand for 5–10 minutes until the yeast has dissolved and starts to foam.

2 Use a wooden spoon to mix in the salt and about one-third of the flour. Mix in another third of the flour, stirring with the spoon until the dough forms a mass and begins to pull away from the sides of the bowl.

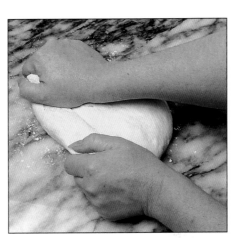

3 Sprinkle some of the remaining flour on to the smooth work surface. Remove the dough from the bowl and begin to knead it, working in the remaining flour a little at a time. Knead for 8–10 minutes. By the end the dough should be elastic and smooth. Form it into a ball.

4 Lightly oil a mixing bowl. Place the dough in the bowl. Stretch a damp tea towel or clear film across the top of the bowl, and leave it to stand in a warm place until the dough has doubled in volume, about 40–50 minutes or more, depending on the type of yeast used. To test whether the dough has risen enough, poke two fingers into the dough. If the indentations remain, the dough is ready to use.

5 Punch the dough down with your fist to release the air. Knead for 1–2 minutes.

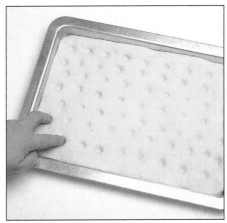

6 Brush a tin with oil. Press the dough into the tin with your fingers to a layer 2.5cm/1in thick. Cover and leave to rise for 30 minutes. Preheat the oven. Make indentations all over the focaccia with your fingers. Brush with oil, add filling and bake until pale golden brown.

Making Scones and Popovers

Scones are quick breads made with a soft dough based on flour and milk, with a raising agent added. Popovers are individual batter puddings, made in a similar way to Yorkshire puddings, then flavoured.

The dough of scones may be rolled out and cut into shapes, it may be dropped from a spoon on to a baking sheet, or lightly patted out and then stamped out with a cutter into rounds or other shapes.

SCONES

1 Sift together the dry ingredients into a large mixing bowl (flour, baking powder with or without bicarbonate of soda, salt, sugar, spices, etc.).

2 Add the fat (butter, margarine or vegetable fat). With a pastry blender or two knives, cut the fat into the dry ingredients until the mixture resembles fine crumbs, or rub into the fat with your fingertips.

3 Add the liquid ingredients (milk, cream, buttermilk, eggs). Stir with a fork until the dry ingredients are thoroughly moistened and will come together in a ball of fairly soft dough in the centre of the bowl.

4 Turn the dough on to a lightly floured surface. Knead it very lightly, folding and pressing to mix evenly, for about 30 seconds. Roll or pat out the dough to a 2cm/1in thickness.

5 With a floured, sharp-edged cutter, cut out rounds or other shapes. Arrange on an ungreased baking sheet. Brush with beaten egg or cream. Bake until golden brown. Serve immediately.

6 For griddle scones: If using a well-seasoned cast iron griddle, there is no need to grease it. Heat it slowly and evenly. Put scone triangles or rounds on the hot griddle and cook for 5–6 minutes on each side or until golden brown and cooked through.

POPOVERS

1 Sift the flour into a large bowl along with other dry ingredients such as salt and ground black pepper. Make a well in the centre of the dry ingredients and put in the eggs, egg yolks and some of the liquid.

2 With a wooden spoon, beat together the eggs and liquid in the well just to mix them. Gradually draw in some of the flour from the sides, stirring vigorously.

3 When the mixture is smooth, stir in the remaining liquid. Stir just until the ingredients are combined – the trick is not to overmix.

4 Pour the mixture into greased muffin tins or ramekins and bake until golden brown. Do not open the oven door during baking time or the popovers may collapse. Run a knife around the edge of each popover to loosen, then turn out and serve hot.

Cutting Tips for Scones

Be sure the cutter or knife is sharp so that the edges of the scone shapes are not compressed; this would prevent rising. Cut the shapes close together so that you won't have to re-roll the dough more than once. If necessary, a short, sturdy drinking glass can be pressed into service as a cutter. Flour the rim well and do not press too hard. When cutting out, don't twist the cutter.

Shaping Rolls

Bread rolls can be made in all sorts of interesting shapes and sizes. Begin by dividing the dough into even-size portions. Try these traditional variations first and then, when you are used to working with dough, experiment with your own customized designs.

1 To shape cottage rolls, divide each portion of dough into two, making one piece about twice the size of the other. Shape both pieces into smooth balls. Dampen the top of the large ball and place the small ball on top. Push a lightly floured index finger through the middle of the dough.

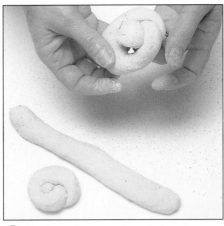

3 To shape knots, roll each dough portion into a fairly long sausage shape. Carefully knot the dough sausage, as you would a piece of string.

5 To shape snipped-top rolls, roll each dough portion into a smooth ball. Using a pair of kitchen scissors, make two or three snips in the top of each ball.

2 To shape clover leaf rolls, divide each portion of dough into three equal pieces. Form each piece into a smooth ball, lightly dampen, and arrange in a clover leaf formation. Lightly press together.

4 To shape plaits, divide each dough portion into three equal pieces. Roll each piece into an even sausage shape. Dampen the three sausages at one end and pinch together. Plait the sausages loosely and pinch together at the other end, dampening lightly first.

6 To shape twists, divide each dough portion into two equal pieces. Roll each piece into an even sausage shape, then twist the two pieces together, dampening at each end and pressing together firmly.

Lining Baking Tins

Ensure that your cakes and teabreads don't stick by lining the tin with greaseproof or non-stick baking paper. Use low fat margarine or oil to lightly grease the tin if necessary.

LINING A ROUND TIN

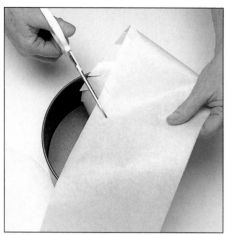

1 To line a round tin, place the tin on greaseproof or non-stick baking paper and draw around the edge. Cut out two circles that size, then cut a strip a little longer than the tin's circumference and one and a half times its depth. Lightly grease the tin and place one paper circle on the base. Make small diagonal cuts along one edge of the paper strip.

2 Put the paper strip inside the tin, with the snipped fringe along the base. Place the second paper circle in the base of the tin, covering the fringe. Grease once more.

LINING A SWISS ROLL TIN

1 To line a Swiss roll tin, cut a piece of non-stick baking paper or greaseproof paper large enough to line the base and sides of the tin. Lay the paper over the tin and make four diagonal cuts, one from each corner of the paper to the nearest corner of the tin.

2 Lightly grease the tin. Place the paper in the tin and smooth into the sides, overlapping the paper corners to fit neatly.

LINING A LOAF TIN

1 To line a loaf tin, measure and cut a strip of greaseproof paper or non-stick baking paper to fit the depth and length of the tin.

2 Lightly grease the tin. Place the strip of paper in the tin so that the paper covers the base and comes up over both long sides. Then press the paper lining into place.

Testing Bread and Cakes

It is very important to check that cakes and bakes are properly cooked, otherwise they can be soggy and cakes may sink in the middle.

TESTING A FRUIT CAKE

1 To test if a fruit cake is ready, push a skewer or cake tester into it; the cake is cooked if the skewer or cake tester comes out clean.

2 Fruit cakes are generally left to cool in the tin for 30 minutes. When cool, turn the cake out carefully, peel away the paper and place on a wire rack or board.

TESTING A SPONGE CAKE

1 To test if a sponge cake is ready, press down lightly in the centre of the cake with your fingertips – if the cake springs back, it is cooked.

2 To remove the cooked sponge cake from the tin, loosen around the edge by carefully scraping around the inside of the tin with a palette knife, invert the cake on to a wire rack, cover with a second rack, then invert again. Remove the top rack and leave to cool.

TESTING BREAD

1 To test if a loaf of bread is ready, first loosen the edges of the loaf with a palette knife, then tip out the loaf.

2 Hold the loaf upside down and tap it gently on the base. If it sounds hollow, the bread is cooked.

Icing a Cake

Confident icing of a cake makes all the difference to its appearance. With just a little practice, your cakes will look completely professional!

MAKING A PIPING BAG

Being able to make your own piping bag is a very handy skill, particularly if you are dealing with small amounts of icing or several colours.

1 Fold a 25cm/10in square of grease-proof paper in half to form a triangle. Using the centre of the long side as the central tip, roll half the paper into a cone.

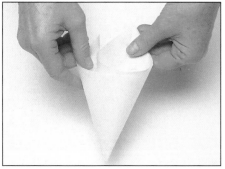

2 Holding the paper in position, continue to roll the other half of the triangle around the first, to form a complete cone.

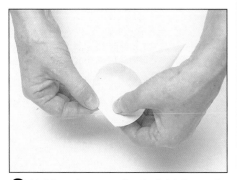

3 Holding the cone firmly, fold the end of the paper triangle over the top into the inside of the cone to secure it. Fill the bag no more than half full with icing, fold over the top several times to seal, then snip off the tip to the required size.

ICING A CAKE

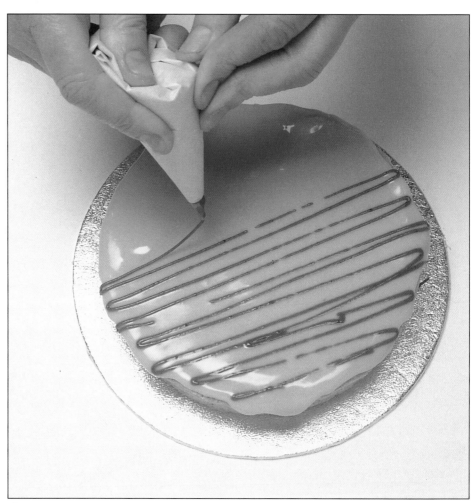

1 To create a simple zig-zag effect, ice the cake all over, then pipe lines in a different colour backwards and forwards over the top.

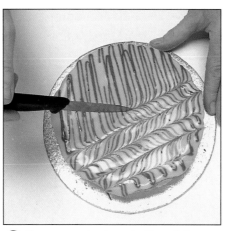

2 To create a feathered effect, follow step 1, then drag a knife through the icing at regular intervals in opposite directions, perpendicular to the lines.

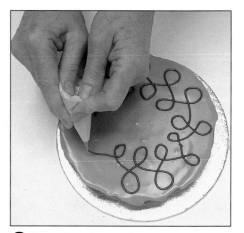

3 To make a figure-of-eight, or a similar effect, ice the cake all over, then, using a different coloured icing, pipe figures of eight around the edge of the cake, in a steady stream.

Preparing Glazes and Citrus Fruits

Apricot glaze is extremely useful for brushing over any kind of fresh fruit topping or filling
to give it a lovely shiny appearance. Oranges, lemons and other citrus fruits are widely used in baking,
both as flavouring and as decoration.

MAKING APRICOT GLAZE

1 Place a few spoonfuls of apricot jam in a small pan, along with a squeeze of lemon juice. Heat the jam, stirring until it is melted and runny.

2 Pour the melted jam into a wire sieve set over a bowl. Stir the jam with a wooden spoon to help it go through.

3 Return the strained jam from the bowl to the pan. Keep the glaze warm and brush it generously over the fresh fruit until evenly coated.

PREPARING CITRUS FRUITS

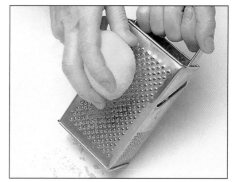

1 To grate the rind from a citrus fruit, use the finest side of the grater. Don't remove any of the white pith and brush off any rind that remains in the grater.

2 To pare the rind from a citrus fruit, use a swivel vegetable peeler. · Remove the rind in strips as if peeling a potato and don't remove any of the white pith.

3 To make citrus rind shreds, or julienne, cut strips of pared rind into very fine shreds using a sharp knife. Boil the shreds for a couple of minutes in water or sugar syrup to soften them.

Low Fat Whipped "Cream"

Serve this sweet "cream" instead of whipped double cream. It isn't suitable for cooking, but freezes very well.

MAKING LOW FAT WHIPPED "CREAM"

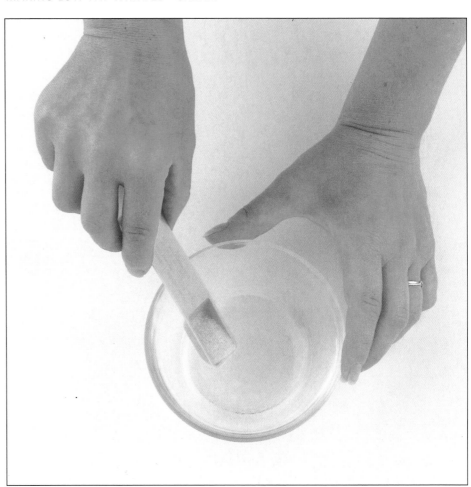

1 Sprinkle the gelatine over 15ml/1 tbsp cold water in a small bowl and leave to "sponge" for 5 minutes. Place the bowl over a saucepan of hot water and stir until dissolved. Leave to cool.

2 Whisk the skimmed milk powder, caster sugar, lemon juice and 60ml/ 4 tbsp cold water until frothy. Add the dissolved gelatine and whisk for a few seconds or more. Chill in the fridge for 30 minutes.

3 Whisk the chilled mixture again until very thick and frothy. Serve within 30 minutes of making.

Using Cream Alternatives
Serve strained yogurt with puddings instead of cream, sweetened with a little honey, if liked. Curd cheese can be used instead of cream.

Making Yogurt and Curd Cheese

Yogurt is an excellent alternative to whipped cream for decorating cakes and desserts.
Strained yogurt and curd cheese are simple to make at home, and tend to be lower in fat
than commercial varieties.

MAKING YOGURT PIPING CREAM

1 Sprinkle the gelatine over 45ml/3 tbsp cold water in a small bowl and leave to
"sponge" for 5 minutes. Place the bowl over a saucepan of hot water and stir until
dissolved. Leave to cool.

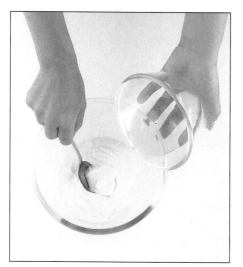

2 Mix together the yogurt, fructose and
vanilla essence. Stir in the gelatine.
Chill in the fridge for 30 minutes, or until
just beginning to set around the edges.

3 Whisk the egg white until stiff and
carefully fold it into the yogurt
mixture. Spoon into a piping bag fitted
with a piping nozzle and use immediately.

MAKING STRAINED YOGURT AND
CURD CHEESE

1 Line a nylon or stainless steel sieve
with a double layer of muslin. Put
over a bowl and pour in the yogurt.

2 Leave to drain in the fridge for
3 hours – it will have separated into
thick strained yogurt and watery whey.

3 For curd cheese, leave to drain in the
fridge for 8 hours or overnight. Spoon
the curd cheese into a bowl, cover and
keep chilled until required.

Cakes

Low in fat doesn't have to
mean low in taste. These
deliciously light cakes
are bursting with flavours
suited to all seasons and
every occasion.

Lemon Chiffon Cake

Lemon mousse provides a tangy filling for this light lemon sponge.

Serves 8
2 eggs
75g/3oz/6 tbsp caster sugar
grated rind of 1 lemon
50g/2oz/½ cup sifted plain flour
lemon shreds, to decorate

For the filling
2 eggs, separated
75g/3oz/6 tbsp caster sugar
grated rind and juice of 1 lemon
30ml/2 tbsp/½ cup water
15ml/1 tbsp gelatine
125ml/4fl oz/½ cup low fat
fromage frais

For the icing
15ml/1 tbsp lemon juice
115g/4oz/scant 1 cup icing sugar, sifted

Cook's Tip
The mousse should be just setting when the egg whites are added. Speed up this process by placing the bowl of mousse in iced water.

NUTRITION NOTES
Per portion
Energy	202Kcals/849kJ
Fat	2.81g
Saturated Fat	0.79g
Cholesterol	96.4mg
Fibre	0.2g

1 Preheat the oven to 180°C/350°F/ Gas 4. Grease and line a 20cm/8in loose-bottomed cake tin. Whisk the eggs, sugar and lemon rind together with a hand-held electric whisk until thick and mousse-like. Gently fold in the flour, then turn the mixture into the prepared tin.

2 Bake for 20–25 minutes until the cake springs back when lightly pressed in the centre. Turn on to a wire rack to cool. Once cold, split the cake in half horizontally and return the lower half to the clean cake tin.

3 Make the filling. Put the egg yolks, sugar, lemon rind and juice in a bowl. Beat with a hand-held electric whisk until thick, pale and creamy.

4 Pour the water into a heatproof bowl and sprinkle the gelatine on top. Leave until spongy, then stir over simmering water until dissolved. Cool, then whisk into the yolk mixture. Fold in the fromage frais. When the mixture begins to set, whisk the egg whites to soft peaks. Fold the egg whites into the mousse mixture.

5 Pour the lemon mousse over the sponge in the cake tin, spreading it to the edges. Set the second layer of sponge on top and chill until set.

6 Slide a palette knife dipped in hot water between the tin and the cake to loosen it. Transfer to a serving plate. To make icing, add enough lemon juice to the icing sugar to make a mixture thick enough to coat the back of a wooden spoon. Pour over the cake and spread to the edges. Decorate with lemon shreds.

Irish Whiskey Cake

This moist, rich fruit cake is drizzled with whiskey as soon as it comes out of the oven.

Serves 12

115g/4oz/⅔ cup glacé cherries
175g/6oz/1 cup dark muscovado sugar
115g/4oz/⅔ cup sultanas
115g/4oz/⅔ cup raisins
115g/4oz/⅔ cup currants
300ml/½ pint/1¼ cups cold tea
300g/10oz/2½ cups self-raising
flour, sifted
1 egg
45ml/3 tbsp Irish whiskey

NUTRITION NOTES

Per portion
Energy   265Kcals/1115kJ
Fat   0.88g
Saturated Fat   0.25g
Cholesterol   16mg
Fibre   1.48g

1 Mix the cherries, sugar, dried fruit and tea in a large bowl. Leave to soak overnight until all the tea has been absorbed into the fruit. Preheat the oven to 180°C/350°F/ Gas 4.

2 Grease and line a 1kg/2¼lb loaf tin. Add the flour, then the egg to the fruit mixture and beat thoroughly until well mixed.

3 Pour the mixture into the prepared tin and bake for 1½ hours or until a skewer inserted into the centre of the cake comes out clean.

4 Prick the top of the cake with a skewer and drizzle over the whiskey while the cake is still hot. Allow to stand for about 5 minutes, then remove from the tin and cool on a wire rack.

Cook's Tip
If time is short, use hot tea and soak the fruit for just 2 hours.

Angel Cake

A delicious light cake to serve as a dessert for a special occasion.

1 Preheat the oven to 180°C/350°F/ Gas 4. Sift both flours on to a sheet of greaseproof paper.

2 Whisk the egg whites in a large clean, dry bowl until very stiff, then gradually add the sugar and vanilla essence, whisking until the mixture is thick and glossy.

3 Gently fold in the flour mixture with a large metal spoon. Spoon into an ungreased 25cm/10in angel cake tin, smooth the surface and bake for about 45–50 minutes, until the cake springs back when lightly pressed.

4 Sprinkle a piece of greaseproof paper with caster sugar and set an egg cup in the centre. Invert the cake tin over the paper, balancing it carefully on the egg cup. When cold, the cake will drop out of the tin. Transfer it to a plate, spoon over the glacé icing, arrange the physalis on top and then dust with icing sugar and serve.

Serves 10
40g/1½oz/⅓ cup cornflour
40g/1½oz/⅓ cup plain flour
8 egg whites
225g/8oz/1 cup caster sugar, plus extra for sprinkling
5ml/1 tsp vanilla essence
90ml/6 tbsp orange-flavoured glacé icing, 4–6 physalis and a little icing sugar, to decorate

NUTRITION NOTES

Per portion
Energy	139Kcals/582kJ
Fat	0.08g
Saturated Fat	0.1g
Cholesterol	0
Fibre	0.13g

Tia Maria Gâteau

A feather-light coffee sponge with a creamy liqueur-flavoured filling.

Serves 8

75g/3oz/¾ cup plain flour
30ml/2 tbsp instant coffee powder
3 eggs
115g/4oz/½ cup caster sugar
coffee beans, to decorate (optional)

For the filling

175g/6oz/¾ cup low fat soft cheese
15ml/1 tbsp clear honey
15ml/1 tbsp Tia Maria liqueur
50g/2oz/¼ cup stem ginger,
roughly chopped

For the icing

225g/8oz/1¾ cups icing sugar, sifted
10ml/2 tsp coffee essence
15ml/1 tbsp water
5ml/1 tsp reduced fat cocoa powder

Cook's Tip
When folding in the flour mixture in step 3, be careful not to remove the air, as it helps the cake to rise.

NUTRITION NOTES

Per portion

Energy	226Kcals/951kJ
Fat	3.14g
Saturated Fat	1.17g
Cholesterol	75.03mg
Fibre	0.64g

1 Preheat the oven to 190°C/375°F/ Gas 5. Grease and line a 20cm/8in deep round cake tin. Sift the flour and coffee powder together on to a sheet of greaseproof paper.

2 Whisk the eggs and sugar in a bowl with a hand-held electric whisk until thick and mousse-like. (When the whisk is lifted, a trail should remain on the surface of the mixture for at least 15 seconds.)

3 Gently fold in the flour mixture with a metal spoon. Turn the mixture into the prepared tin. Bake the sponge for 30–35 minutes or until it springs back when lightly pressed. Turn on to a wire rack to cool completely.

4 To make the filling, mix the soft cheese with the honey in a bowl. Beat until smooth, then stir in the Tia Maria and chopped stem ginger.

5 Split the cake in half horizontally and sandwich the two halves together with the Tia Maria filling.

6 Make the icing. In a bowl, mix the icing sugar and coffee essence with enough of the water to make a consistency that will coat the back of a wooden spoon. Pour three-quarters of the icing over the cake, spreading it evenly to the edges. Stir the cocoa into the remaining icing until smooth. Spoon into a piping bag fitted with a writing nozzle and pipe the mocha icing over the coffee icing. Decorate with coffee beans, if liked.

Chocolate Banana Cake

A chocolate cake that's deliciously low in fat – it is moist enough to eat without the icing
if you want to cut down on calories.

Serves 8

225g/8oz/2 cups self-raising flour
45ml/3 tbsp fat-reduced cocoa powder
115g/4oz/⅔ cup light muscovado sugar
30ml/2 tbsp malt extract
30ml/2 tbsp golden syrup
2 eggs
60ml/4 tbsp skimmed milk
60ml/4 tbsp sunflower oil
2 large ripe bananas

For the icing

225g/8oz/2 cups icing
sugar, sifted
35ml/7 tsp fat-reduced cocoa
powder, sifted
15–30ml/1–2 tbsp warm water

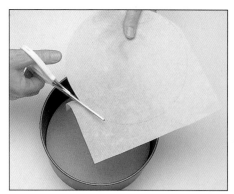

1 Preheat the oven to 160°C/325°F/ Gas 3. Grease and line a deep round 20cm/8in cake tin.

2 Sift the flour into a mixing bowl with the cocoa powder. Stir in the sugar.

3 Make a well in the centre and add the malt extract, golden syrup, eggs, milk and oil. Mash the bananas thoroughly and stir them into the mixture until thoroughly combined.

4 Pour the cake mixture into the prepared tin and bake for 1–1¼ hours or until the centre of the cake springs back when lightly pressed.

5 Remove the cake from the tin and leave on a wire rack to cool.

6 Reserve 50g/2oz/⅓ cup icing sugar and 5ml/1 tsp cocoa powder. Make a dark icing by beating the remaining sugar and cocoa powder with enough of the warm water to make a thick icing. Pour it over the top of the cake and spread evenly to the edges. Make a thinner, lighter icing by mixing the remaining icing sugar and cocoa powder with a few drops of water. Drizzle or pipe this icing across the top of the cake to decorate.

NUTRITION NOTES

Per portion

Energy	411Kcals/1727kJ
Fat	8.791g
Saturated Fat	2.06g
Cholesterol	48.27mg
Fibre	2.06g

Coffee Sponge Drops

These are delicious on their own, but taste even better with a filling made by mixing low fat soft cheese with drained and chopped stem ginger.

Makes 12
50g/2oz/½ cup plain flour
15ml/1 tbsp instant coffee powder
2 eggs
75g/3oz/6 tbsp caster sugar

For the filling
115g/4oz/½ cup low fat soft cheese
40g/1½oz/¼ cup chopped stem ginger

1 Preheat the oven to 190°C/375°F/ Gas 5. Line two baking sheets with non-stick baking paper. Make the filling by beating together the soft cheese and stem ginger. Chill until required. Sift the flour and instant coffee powder together.

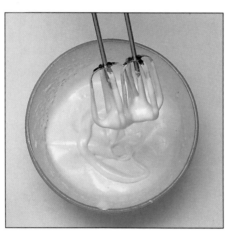

2 Combine the eggs and caster sugar in a bowl. Beat with a hand-held electric whisk until thick and mousse-like. (When the whisk is lifted, a trail should remain on the surface of the mixture for at least 15 seconds.)

3 Carefully add the sifted flour and coffee mixture and gently fold in with a metal spoon, being careful not to knock out any air.

4 Spoon the mixture into a piping bag fitted with a 1cm/½in plain nozzle. Pipe 4cm/1½in rounds on the baking sheets. Bake for 12 minutes. Cool on a wire rack, then sandwich together with the filling.

Cook's Tip
As an alternative to stem ginger in the filling, try walnuts.

NUTRITION NOTES
Per portion
Energy	69Kcals/290kJ
Fat	1.36g
Saturated Fat	0.5g
Cholesterol	33.33mg
Fibre	0.29g

Chocolate and Orange Angel Cake

This light-as-air sponge with its fluffy icing is virtually fat free, yet tastes heavenly.

Serves 10
25g/1oz/¼ cup plain flour
15g/½oz/2 tbsp reduced fat
cocoa powder
15g/½oz/2 tbsp cornflour
pinch of salt
5 egg whites
2.5ml/½ tsp cream of tartar
115g/4oz/scant ½ cup caster sugar
blanched and shredded rind of
1 orange, to decorate

For the icing
200g/7oz/1 cup caster sugar
1 egg white

1 Preheat the oven to 180°C/350°F/ Gas 4. Sift the flour, cocoa powder, cornflour and salt together three times. Beat the egg whites in a large clean, dry bowl until foamy. Add the cream of tartar, then whisk until soft peaks form.

2 Add the caster sugar to the egg whites a spoonful at a time, whisking after each addition. Sift a third of the flour and cocoa mixture over the meringue and gently fold in. Repeat, sifting and folding in the flour and cocoa mixture two more times.

3 Spoon the mixture into a non-stick 20cm/8in ring mould and level the top. Bake for 35 minutes or until springy to the touch. Turn upside down on to a wire rack and leave to cool in the tin. Carefully ease out of the tin.

4 For the icing, put the sugar in a pan with 75ml/5 tbsp cold water. Stir over a low heat until dissolved. Boil until the syrup reaches a temperature of 120°C/ 240°F on a sugar thermometer or when a drop of the syrup makes a soft ball when dripped into a cup of cold water. Remove from the heat.

5 Whisk the egg white until stiff. Add the syrup in a thin stream, whisking all the time. Continue to whisk until the mixture is very thick and fluffy.

6 Spread the icing over the top and sides of the cooled cake. Sprinkle the orange rind over the top of the cake and serve.

NUTRITION NOTES
Per portion
Energy	153Kcals/644kJ
Fat	0.27g
Saturated Fat	0.13g
Cholesterol	0
Fibre	0.25g

Apricot and Orange Roulade

This elegant dessert is very good served with a spoonful of natural yogurt or crème fraîche.

Serves 6

4 egg whites
115g/4oz/½ cup golden caster sugar
50g/2oz/½ cup plain flour
finely grated rind of 1 small orange
45ml/3 tbsp orange juice
10ml/2 tsp icing sugar and shreds of
orange zest, to decorate

For the filling

115g/4oz/⅔ cup ready-to-eat dried apricots
115g/4oz/⅔ cup orange juice

NUTRITION NOTES

Per portion

Energy	203Kcals/853kJ
Fat	10.52g
Saturated Fat	2.05g
Cholesterol	0
Fibre	2.53g

1 Preheat the oven to 200°C/400°F/ Gas 6. Grease a 23 x 33cm/9 x 13in Swiss roll tin and line it with non-stick baking paper. Grease the paper.

2 For the roulade, place the egg whites in a large bowl and whisk them until they hold peaks. Gradually add the sugar, whisking hard between each addition.

3 Fold in the flour, orange rind and juice. Spoon the mixture into the prepared tin and spread it evenly.

4 Bake for about 15–18 minutes, or until the sponge is firm and light golden in colour. Turn out on to a sheet of non-stick baking paper and roll it up Swiss roll-style loosely from one short side. Leave to cool.

5 For the filling, roughly chop the apricots, and place them in a saucepan with the orange juice. Cover the tin and leave to simmer until most of the liquid has been absorbed. Purée the apricots in a food processor or blender.

6 Unroll the roulade and spread with the apricot mixture. Roll up, arrange strips of paper diagonally across the roll, sprinkle lightly with lines of icing sugar, remove the paper and scatter with orange zest to serve.

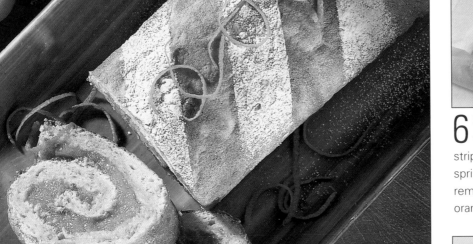

Cook's Tip

Make and bake the sponge mixture a day in advance and keep it, rolled with the paper, in a cool place. Fill it with the fruit purée 2–3 hours before serving. The sponge can also be frozen for up to 2 months; thaw it at room temperature and fill it as above.

Nectarine Amaretto Cake

Amaretto liqueur adds a hint of luxury to this fruity cake.

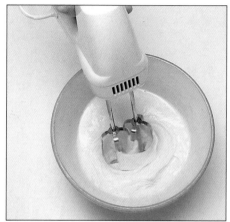

1 Preheat the oven to 180°C/350°F/ Gas 4. Grease a 20cm/8in round, loose-bottomed cake tin. Whisk together the egg yolks, caster sugar, lemon rind and juice in a bowl until the mixture is thick, pale and creamy.

2 Fold in the semolina, almonds and flour until smooth.

3 Whisk the egg whites in a bowl until fairly stiff. Use a metal spoon to stir a generous spoonful of the whites into the semolina mixture, then fold in the remaining egg whites. Spoon the mixture into the cake tin.

4 Bake for 30–35 minutes until the centre of the cake springs back when pressed lightly. Remove from the oven and loosen around the edge with a palette knife. Prick the top with a skewer. Leave to cool in the tin.

5 To make the syrup, heat the sugar and water in a small pan, stirring until the sugar is dissolved. Boil without stirring for 2 minutes. Add the Amaretto liqueur and drizzle the liqueur syrup over the cake in the tin.

6 Remove the cake from the tin and transfer to a serving plate. Decorate with sliced nectarines. Brush with warm apricot glaze.

Serves 8

3 eggs, separated
175g/6oz/¾ cup caster sugar
grated rind and juice of 1 lemon
50g/2oz/⅓ cup semolina
25g/1oz/¼ cup ground almonds
25g/1oz/¼ cup plain flour
2 nectarines, halved and stoned
60ml/4 tbsp apricot glaze

For the syrup

45g/3oz/⅓ cup caster sugar
90ml/6 tbsp water
30ml/2 tbsp Amaretto liqueur

NUTRITION NOTES

Per portion
Energy	264Kcals/1108kJ
Fat	5.7g
Saturated Fat	0.85g
Cholesterol	72.19mg
Fibre	1.08g

Banana and Gingerbread Slices

Very quick to make and deliciously moist due to the addition of bananas.

Serves 20

275g/10oz/2 cups plain flour
20ml/4 tsp ground ginger
10ml/2 tsp mixed spice
5ml/1 tsp bicarbonate of soda
115g/4oz/½ cup soft light brown sugar
60ml/4 tbsp sunflower oil
30ml/2 tbsp molasses or black treacle
30ml/2 tbsp malt extract
2 eggs
60ml/4 tbsp orange juice
3 bananas
115g/4oz/⅔ cup raisins

Variation

To make Spiced Honey and Banana Cake; omit the ground ginger and add another 5ml/1 tsp mixed spice; omit the malt extract and the molasses or treacle and add 60ml/4 tbsp strong-flavoured clear honey instead; and replace the raisins with either sultanas, coarsely chopped ready-to-eat dried apricots, or semi-dried pineapple. If you choose to use the pineapple, then you could also replace the orange juice with fresh pineapple juice.

Cook's Tip

The flavour of this cake develops as it keeps, so if you can, store it for a few days before eating.

NUTRITION NOTES

Per portion

Energy	148Kcals/621kJ
Fat	3.07g
Saturated Fat	0.53g
Cholesterol	19.3mg
Fibre	0.79g

1 Preheat the oven to 180°C/350°F/ Gas 4. Lightly grease and line an 18 x 28cm/7 x 11in baking tin.

2 Sift the flour into a bowl with the spices and bicarbonate of soda. Mix in the sugar with some of the flour and sift it all into the bowl.

3 Make a well in the centre, add the oil, molasses or black treacle, malt extract, eggs and orange juice and mix together thoroughly.

4 Mash the bananas, then add them to the bowl with the raisins and mix together well.

5 Pour the mixture into the prepared baking tin and bake for about 35–40 minutes, or until the centre springs back when lightly pressed.

6 Leave the cake in the tin to cool for 5 minutes, then turn out on to a wire rack and leave to cool completely. Cut into 20 slices.

Banana Ginger Parkin

Parkin keeps well and really improves over time. Store it in a covered container for up to two months.

Serves 12

200g/7oz/1¾ cups plain flour
10ml/2 tsp bicarbonate of soda
10ml/2 tsp ground ginger
150g/5oz/1¾ cups medium oatmeal
60ml/4 tbsp dark muscovado sugar
75g/3oz/6 tbsp sunflower margarine
150g/5oz/⅔ cup golden syrup
1 egg, beaten
3 ripe bananas, mashed
75g/3oz/¾ cup icing sugar
stem ginger, to decorate

NUTRITION NOTES

Per portion

Energy	277Kcals/1163kJ
Fat	6.9g
Saturated Fat	6.9g
Cholesterol	16.4mg
Fibre	1.72g

1 Preheat the oven to 160°C/325°F/ Gas 3. Grease and line an 18 x 28cm/ 7 x 11in cake tin.

2 Sift together the flour, bicarbonate of soda and ginger, then stir in the oatmeal. Melt the sugar, margarine and syrup in a saucepan, then stir into the flour mixture. Beat in the egg and mashed bananas.

3 Spoon into the tin and bake for about 1 hour, or until firm to the touch. Allow to cool in the tin, then turn out and cut into squares.

4 Sift the icing sugar into a bowl and stir in just enough water to make a smooth, runny icing. Drizzle the icing over each square and top with a piece of stem ginger, to decorate.

Cook's Tip

This is a nutritious, energy-giving cake that is a really good choice for packed lunches as it doesn't break up too easily.

Spiced Date and Walnut Cake

A classic flavour combination, which makes a very easy low fat, high-fibre cake.

1 Preheat the oven to 180°C/350°F/ Gas 4. Grease and line a 900g/2lb loaf tin with greaseproof paper.

2 Sift together the flour and spice, adding back any bran from the sieve. Stir in the dates and walnuts.

3 Mix the oil, sugar and milk, then stir evenly into the dry ingredients.

4 Spoon into the prepared tin and arrange the walnut halves on top. Bake the cake in the oven for about 45–50 minutes, or until golden brown and firm. Turn out the cake, remove the lining paper and leave to cool on a wire rack.

Serves 10

300g/11oz/2½ cups
wholemeal self-raising flour
10ml/2 tsp mixed spice
150g/5oz/¾ cup chopped dates
50g/2oz/½ cup chopped walnuts
60ml/4 tbsp sunflower oil
115g/4oz/½ cup dark muscovado sugar
300ml/½ pint/1¼ cups skimmed milk
walnut halves, to decorate

NUTRITION NOTES
Per portion
Energy	265Kcals/1114kJ
Fat	9.27g
Saturated Fat	1.14g
Cholesterol	0.6mg
Fibre	3.51g

Cook's Tip
Pecan nuts can be used in place of the walnuts in this cake.

Greek Honey and Lemon Cake

Moist and tangy, a delicious tea-time treat.

Makes 16 slices

40g/1½oz/3 tbsp sunflower margarine
60ml/4 tbsp clear honey
finely grated rind and juice of 1 lemon
150ml/¼ pint/⅔ cup skimmed milk
150g/5oz/1¼ cups plain flour
7.5ml/1½ tsp baking powder
2.5ml/½ tsp grated nutmeg
50g/2oz/¼ cup semolina
2 egg whites
10ml/2 tsp sesame seeds

NUTRITION NOTES

Per portion

Energy	82Kcals/342kJ
Fat	2.62g
Saturated Fat	0.46g
Cholesterol	0.36mg
Fibre	0.41g

1 Preheat the oven to 200°C/400°F/ Gas 6. Lightly oil a 19cm/7½in square deep cake tin and line the base with non-stick baking paper.

2 Place the margarine and 45ml/3 tbsp of the honey in a saucepan and heat gently until melted. Reserve 15ml/1 tbsp lemon juice, then stir in the rest with the lemon rind and milk.

3 Sift together the flour, baking powder and nutmeg. Gradually beat the semolina into the mixture. Whisk the egg whites until they form soft peaks, then fold evenly into the mixture.

4 Spoon into the tin and sprinkle with sesame seeds. Bake for 25–30 minutes, until golden brown. Mix together the reserved honey and lemon juice and drizzle over the cake while warm. Cool in the tin, then cut into fingers to serve.

Strawberry Roulade

A creamy fruit filling is delicious in a light roulade.

1 Preheat the oven to 200°C/400°F/ Gas 6. Oil a 23 x 33cm/9 x 13in Swiss roll tin and line with non-stick baking paper.

2 Place the egg whites in a large bowl and whisk until they form soft peaks. Gradually whisk in the sugar. Fold in half of the sifted flour, then fold in the rest with the orange juice.

3 Spoon the mixture into the prepared tin, spreading evenly. Bake for 15–18 minutes, or until golden brown and firm to the touch.

4 Meanwhile, spread out a sheet of non-stick baking paper and sprinkle with caster sugar. Turn out the cake on to this and remove the lining paper. Roll up the sponge loosely from one short side, with the paper inside. Cool.

5 Unroll and remove the paper. Stir the strawberries into the fromage frais and spread over the sponge. Re-roll and serve decorated with strawberries.

Serves 6

4 egg whites
115g/4oz/⅔ cup golden caster sugar
75g/3oz/⅔ cup plain flour, sifted
30ml/2 tbsp orange juice
caster sugar, for sprinkling
115g/4oz/1 cup strawberries, chopped
150g/5oz/¾ cup low fat fromage frais
strawberries, to decorate

NUTRITION NOTES

Per portion

Energy	154Kcals/646kJ
Fat	0.24g
Saturated Fat	0.01g
Cholesterol	0.25mg
Fibre	0.61g

Peach Swiss Roll

A feather-light sponge enclosing peach jam – delicious at tea time.

Serves 6–8

3 eggs
115g/4oz/½ cup caster sugar, plus extra for sprinkling
75g/3oz/¾ cup plain flour, sifted
15ml/1 tbsp boiling water
90ml/6 tbsp peach jam
icing sugar, for dusting (optional)

Cook's Tip

To decorate the Swiss roll with glacé icing, make the icing with 115g/4oz/1¾ cup icing sugar and enough warm water to make a thin glacé icing. Put in a piping bag fitted with a small writing nozzle and pipe lines over the top.

NUTRITION NOTES

Per portion

Energy	178Kcals/746kJ
Fat	2.54g
Saturated Fat	0.67g
Cholesterol	82.5mg
Fibre	0.33g

1 Preheat the oven to 200°C/400°F/ Gas 6. Grease a 320 x 20cm/12x 8in Swiss roll tin and line with non-stick baking paper. Combine the eggs and sugar in a bowl. Beat with a hand-held electric whisk until thick and mousse-like. (When the whisk is lifted, a trail should remain on the surface of the mixture for at least 15 seconds.)

2 Carefully fold in the flour with a large metal spoon, then add the boiling water in the same way.

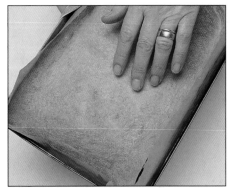

3 Spoon into the prepared tin, spread evenly to the edges and bake for about 10–12 minutes until the cake springs back when lightly pressed.

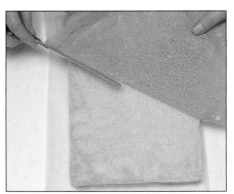

4 Spread a sheet of greaseproof paper on a flat surface, sprinkle it with caster sugar, then invert the cake on top. Peel off the lining paper.

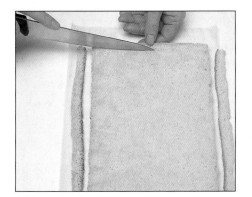

5 Neatly trim the edges of the cake. Make a neat cut two-thirds of the way through the cake, about 1cm/½in from the short edge nearest you.

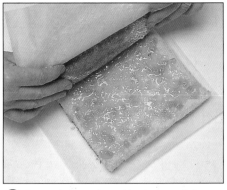

6 Spread the cake with the peach jam and roll up quickly from the partially cut end. Hold in position for a minute, making sure the join is underneath. Cool on a wire rack. Decorate with glacé icing (see Cook's Tip) or dust with icing sugar before serving.

Spiced Apple Cake

Grated apple and chopped dates give this cake a natural sweetness.

Serves 8

225g/8oz/2 cups self-raising
wholemeal flour
5ml/1 tsp baking powder
10ml/2 tsp ground cinnamon
175g/6oz/1 cup chopped dates
75g/3oz/½ cup light muscovado sugar
15ml/1 tbsp pear and apple spread
120ml/4fl oz/½ cup apple juice
2 eggs
90ml/6 tbsp sunflower oil
2 eating apples, cored and grated
15ml/1 tbsp chopped walnuts

NUTRITION NOTES

Per portion
Energy	331Kcals/13895kJ
Fat	11.41g
Saturated Fat	1.68g
Cholesterol	48.13mg
Fibre	2.5g

1 Preheat the oven to 180°C/350°F/ Gas 4. Grease and line a deep round 20cm/8in cake tin. Sift the flour, baking powder and cinnamon into a mixing bowl, then mix in the dates and make a well in the centre.

2 Mix the sugar with the pear and apple spread in a small bowl. Gradually stir in the apple juice. Add to the dry ingredients with the eggs, oil and grated apples. Mix thoroughly.

3 Spoon the mixture into the prepared cake tin, sprinkle liberally with the walnuts and bake for 60–65 minutes or until a skewer inserted into the centre of the cake comes out clean. Transfer to a wire rack, remove the lining paper and leave to cool.

Cook's Tip
Omit 25g/1oz/2 tbsp sugar if the fruit is very sweet. It is not necessary to peel the apples – the skin adds extra fibre and softens on cooking.

Fruit and Nut Cake

A rich fruit cake that improves with keeping.

1 Preheat the oven to 160°C/325°F/ Gas 3. Grease and line a deep round 20cm/8in cake tin. Secure a band of brown paper around the outside.

4 Turn the mixture into the prepared tin and smooth the surface. Arrange the almonds and cherries in a pattern over the top. Bake for 2 hours or until a skewer comes out clean. Transfer to a wire rack until cold, then lift out of the tin and remove the paper.

Serves 12–14

175g/6oz/1½ cups self-raising wholemeal flour
175g/6oz/1½ cups self-raising white flour
10ml/2 tsp mixed spice
15ml/1 tbsp apple and apricot spread
45ml/3 tbsp clear honey
15ml/1 tbsp molasses or black treacle
90ml/6 tbsp sunflower oil
175ml/6fl oz/¾ cup orange juice
2 eggs, beaten
675g/1½lb/4 cups luxury mixed dried fruit
45ml/3 tbsp split almonds
50g/2oz/½ cup glacé cherries, halved

NUTRITION NOTES

Per portion

Energy	333Kcals/14000kJ
Fat	8.54g
Saturated Fat	1.12g
Cholesterol	29.62mg
Fibre	3.08g

2 Sift the flours into a mixing bowl together with the mixed spice and make a well in the centre.

3 Put the apple and apricot spread in a small bowl. Gradually stir in the honey and molasses or treacle. Add to the dry ingredients with the oil, orange juice, eggs and mixed fruit. Mix thoroughly.

Eggless Christmas Cake

A deliciously clever way to create a low-calorie Christmas treat!

Serves 12

75g/3oz/½ cup sultanas
75g/3oz/½ cup raisins
75g/3oz/⅔ cup currants
75g/3oz/½ cup cut glacé
cherries, halved
50g/2oz/⅓ cup cut mixed peel
250ml/8fl oz/1 cup apple juice
25g/1oz/¼ cup toasted hazelnuts
30ml/2 tbsp pumpkin seeds
2 pieces stem ginger in syrup, chopped
finely grated rind of 1 lemon
120ml/4fl oz/½ cup skimmed milk
120ml/4fl oz/½ cup sunflower oil
225g/8oz/2 cups wholemeal self-
raising flour
10ml/2 tsp mixed spice
45ml/3 tbsp brandy or dark rum
apricot jam, for brushing
glacé fruits, to decorate

1 Place the sultanas, raisins, currants, cherries and mixed peel in a bowl and stir in the apple juice. Cover and leave to soak overnight.

2 Preheat the oven to 150°C/300°F/Gas 2.

3 Lightly grease and line an 18cm/7in square cake tin.

4 Add the hazelnuts, pumpkin seeds, ginger and lemon rind to the soaked fruit. Stir in the milk and oil. Sift the flour and spice. Stir in with the brandy or rum.

5 Spoon into the prepared tin and bake for 1½ hours, or until golden brown and firm to the touch. Turn out and cool on a wire rack. Brush with sieved apricot jam and decorate with glacé fruits.

NUTRITION NOTES

Per portion	
Energy	225Kcals/946kJ
Fat	6.13g
Saturated Fat	0.89g
Cholesterol	0.2mg
Fibre	2.45g

Cranberry and Apple Ring

Tangy cranberries add an unusual flavour to this low fat cake. It is best eaten very fresh.

1 Preheat the oven to 180°C/350°F/ Gas 4. Lightly grease a 1 litre/1¾ pint/ 4 cup ring mould with oil.

2 Sift together the flour and ground cinnamon, then stir in the sugar.

3 Toss together the diced apple and cranberries. Stir into the dry ingredients, then add the oil and apple juice and beat well.

4 Spoon the mixture into the prepared ring mould and bake for about 35–40 minutes, or until the cake is firm to the touch. Turn out and leave to cool completely on a wire rack.

5 To serve, drizzle warmed cranberry jelly over the cake and decorate with apple slices.

Serves 8

225g/8oz/2 cups self-raising flour
5ml/1 tsp ground cinnamon
75g/3oz/½ cup light muscovado sugar
1 crisp eating apple, cored and diced
75g/3oz/½ cup fresh or
frozen cranberries
60ml/4 tbsp sunflower oil
150ml/¾ pint/⅔ cup apple juice
cranberry jelly and apple slices,
to decorate

NUTRITION NOTES

Per portion
Energy	202Kcals/848kJ
Fat	5.91g
Saturated Fat	0.76g
Cholesterol	0
Fibre	1.55g

Cook's Tip
Fresh cranberries are available throughout the winter months and if you don't use them all at once, they can be frozen for up to a year.

Carrot Cake with Lemon Frosting

Lemon frosting is the perfect topping for this all-time favourite.

Serves 8

225g/8oz/2 cups wholemeal
self-raising flour
10ml/2 tsp ground allspice
115g/4oz/⅔ cup light muscovado sugar
2 medium carrots, grated
50g/2oz/⅓ cup sultanas
75ml/5 tbsp sunflower oil
75ml/5 tbsp orange juice
75ml/5 tbsp skimmed milk
2 egg whites

For the frosting

175g/6oz/¾ cup skimmed
milk soft cheese
finely grated rind of ½ lemon
30ml/2 tbsp clear honey
shreds of lemon rind, to decorate

NUTRITION NOTES

Per portion
Energy	272Kcals/1146kJ
Fat	7.72g
Saturated Fat	1.04g
Cholesterol	0.4mg
Fibre	3.33g

1 Preheat the oven to 180°C/350°F/ Gas 4. Grease a deep 18cm/7in round cake tin and line the base with non-stick baking paper.

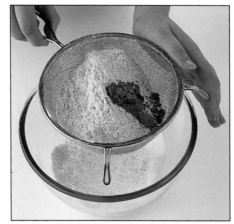

2 Sift the flour and spice, then stir in the sugar, grated carrots and sultanas.

3 Mix the liquids, then stir into the dry ingredients. Whisk the egg whites until stiff, then fold in evenly. Spoon into the tin and bake for 45–50 minutes.

4 Turn out and cool. For the frosting, beat together the cheese, lemon rind and honey until smooth. Spread over the top of the cooled cake, swirling with a palette knife. Decorate with lemon rind.

Chewy Fruit Muesli Slice

Low in fat and high in fibre . . . and delicious as well.

1 Preheat the oven to 190°C/375°F/
Gas 5. Place all the ingredients in
a large bowl and mix well. Press the
mixture into a 20cm/8in round, non-stick
sandwich tin and bake for 35–40 minutes,
or until lightly browned and firm.

2 Mark the muesli slice into wedges
and leave to cool in the tin.

Makes 8 slices

75g/3oz/½ cup ready-to-eat dried
apricots, chopped
1 eating apple, cored and grated
150g/5oz/1¼ cups Swiss-style muesli
150ml/¼ pint/⅔ cup apple juice
15g/½oz/1 tbsp soft
sunflower margarine

NUTRITION NOTES
Per portion

Energy	112Kcals/467kJ
Fat	2.75g
Saturated Fat	0.48g
Cholesterol	0.13mg
Fibre	2.09g

Ginger Cake with Spiced Cream

A spicy and comforting cake, ideal for winter evenings.

Serves 9

175g/6oz/1½ cups plain flour
10ml/2 tsp baking powder
2.5ml/½ tsp salt
10ml/2 tsp ground ginger
10ml/2 tsp ground cinnamon
5ml/1 tsp ground cloves
1.5ml/¼ tsp ground nutmeg
2 eggs
200g/7oz/1 cup granulated sugar
250ml/8fl oz/1 cup whipping cream
5ml/1 tsp vanilla essence
icing sugar, to decorate

For the spiced whipped cream

175ml/6fl oz/¾ cup low fat
whipping cream
5ml/1 tsp icing sugar
1.25ml/¼ tsp ground cinnamon
1.25ml/¼ tsp ground ginger
0.75ml/⅛ tsp grated nutmeg

1 Preheat the oven to 180°C/350°F/ Gas 4. Grease a 23cm/9in square baking tin.

2 Sift the flour, baking powder, salt, ginger, cinnamon, cloves and nutmeg into a bowl. Set aside.

3 With an electric mixer, beat the eggs on a high speed until very thick, for about 5 minutes. Gradually beat in the granulated sugar.

4 With the mixer on a low speed, beat in the flour mixture alternately with the cream into the eggs, beginning and ending with the flour. Stir in the vanilla.

5 Pour into the tin and bake until the top springs back when touched lightly, for 35–40 minutes. Leave to cool in the tin on a wire rack for 10 minutes.

6 To make the spiced whipped cream, combine the ingredients in a bowl and whip until the cream holds soft peaks. Sprinkle icing sugar over the hot cake, cut into nine squares and serve with the spiced whipped cream.

NUTRITION NOTES

Per portion

Energy	305Kcals/1282kJ
Fat	11.6g
Saturated Fat	6.6g
Cholesterol	69mg
Fibre	0.8g

Apple and Pear Skillet Cake

An unusual but delicious cake, prepared on the hob and then baked in the oven.

1 Preheat the oven to 190°C/375°F/
Gas 5. In a mixing bowl, toss together
the apple slices, pear slices, walnuts,
cinnamon and nutmeg. Set aside.

2 With an electric mixer, beat together
the eggs, flour, brown sugar, milk
and vanilla.

3 Melt the butter or margarine in a
23cm or 25cm/9in or 10in ovenproof
skillet (preferably cast iron) over a
medium heat. Add the apple mixture.
Cook until lightly caramelized, for about
5 minutes, stirring occasionally.

4 Pour the batter over the fruit and
nuts. Transfer the skillet to the oven
and bake for about 30 minutes, until the
cake is puffy and pulling away from the
sides of the pan.

5 Sprinkle the cake lightly with icing
sugar and serve hot.

Serves 6

1 apple, peeled, cored and thinly sliced
1 pear, peeled, cored and thinly sliced
50g/2oz/½ cup walnut pieces, chopped
5ml/1 tsp ground cinnamon
5ml/1 tsp grated nutmeg
3 eggs
75g/3oz/¾ cup plain flour
30ml/2 tbsp light brown sugar,
firmly packed
6fl oz/¾ cup skimmed milk
5ml/1 tsp vanilla essence
60ml/4 tbsp butter or margarine
icing sugar, for sprinkling

NUTRITION NOTES
Per portion

Energy	315Kcals/1311kJ
Fat	19.9g
Saturated Fat	3.3g
Cholesterol	98mg
Fibre	1.8g

Cinnamon Apple Gâteau

Make this lovely cake for an autumn celebration.

Serves 6
3 eggs
115g/4oz/½ cup caster sugar
75g/3oz/¾ cup plain flour
5ml/1 tsp ground cinnamon

For the filling and topping
4 large eating apples
50ml/4 tbsp clear honey
15ml/1 tbsp water
75g/3oz/½ cup sultanas
2.5ml/½ tsp ground cinnamon
350g/12oz/1½ cups low fat soft cheese
40ml/4 tbsp reduced fat fromage frais
10ml/2 tsp lemon juice
45ml/3 tbsp apricot glaze
mint sprigs, to decorate

Cook's Tip
Apricot glaze is useful for brushing over a fresh fruit topping or filling. Place a few spoonfuls of apricot jam in a small pan along with a squeeze of lemon juice. Heat the jam, stirring until it is melted and runny. Pour the melted jam into a wire sieve set over a bowl. Stir the jam with a wooden spoon to help it go through. Return the strained jam to the pan. Keep the glaze warm until needed.

NUTRITION NOTES
Per portion

Energy	203Kcals/853kJ
Fat	10.52g
Saturated Fat	2.05g
Cholesterol	0
Fibre	2.53g

1 Preheat the oven to 190°C/375°F/ Gas 5. Grease and line a 23cm/9in sandwich cake tin. Place the eggs and caster sugar in a bowl and beat with a hand-held electric whisk until thick and mousse-like. (When the whisk is lifted, a trail should remain on the surface of the mixture for at least 15 seconds.)

2 Sift the flour and cinnamon over the egg mixture and fold in with a large metal spoon. Pour into the prepared tin and bake for 25–30 minutes or until the cake springs back when lightly pressed. Turn the cake on to a wire rack to cool.

3 To make the filling, peel, core and slice three of the apples and put them in a saucepan. Add 30ml/2 tbsp of the honey and the water. Cover and cook over a gentle heat for about 10 minutes. Add the sultanas and cinnamon, stir well, replace the lid and leave to cool.

4 Put the soft cheese in a bowl with the remaining honey, the fromage frais and half the lemon juice. Beat until the mixture is smooth.

5 Halve the cake horizontally, place the bottom half on a board and drizzle over any liquid from the apples. Spread with two-thirds of the cheese mixture, then top with the apple filling. Fit the top of the cake in place.

6 Swirl the remaining cheese mixture over the top of the sponge. Core and slice the remaining apple, sprinkle with lemon juice and use to decorate the edge of the cake. Brush the apple with the apricot glaze and place mint sprigs on top, to decorate.

Scones, Muffins, Buns and Biscuits

Served warm and straight from the oven, these bite-size bakes are a pleasure for the palate – with the added health benefit of reduced-fat content.

Blueberry Muffins

A real old favourite – and they are not high in calories or fat.

Makes 12

150g/5oz/1¼ cups plain flour
50g/2oz/⅓ cup granulated sugar
10ml/2 tsp baking powder
2.5ml/½ tsp salt
2 eggs
60ml/4 tbsp butter, melted
175ml/6fl oz/¾ cup skimmed milk
5ml/1 tsp vanilla essence
5ml/1 tsp grated lemon rind
115g/4oz/1 cup fresh blueberries

NUTRITION NOTES

Per portion

Energy	124Kcals/524kJ
Fat	3.9g
Saturated Fat	0.8g
Cholesterol	33mg
Fibre	0.8g

1 Preheat the oven to 200°C/400°F/ Gas 6.

2 Grease a 12-cup muffin tin or use paper liners.

3 Sift the flour, sugar, baking powder and salt into a bowl.

4 In another bowl, whisk the eggs until blended. Add the melted butter, milk, vanilla essence and lemon rind and stir to combine. Make a well in the dry ingredients and pour in the egg mixture. With a large metal spoon, stir just until the flour is moistened, not until smooth.

5 Fold in the blueberries.

6 Spoon the batter into the cups, leaving room for the muffins to rise. Bake for 20–25 minutes, or until well risen and firm in the middle. Allow to cool in the tin for about 5 minutes before turning out.

Apple Cranberry Muffins

Fruit and nuts are a winning combination in these mouthwatering muffins.

1 Preheat the oven to 180°C/350°F/ Gas 4. Grease a 12-cup muffin tin or use paper liners.

2 Melt the butter or margarine over gentle heat. Set aside to cool.

3 Place the egg in a mixing bowl and whisk lightly. Add the melted butter or margarine and whisk to combine.

4 Add the sugar, orange rind and juice. Whisk to blend, then set aside. In a large bowl, sift together the flour, baking powder, bicarbonate of soda, cinnamon, nutmeg, allspice, ginger and salt. Set aside.

5 Quarter, core and peel the apples. Then dice coarsely, using a sharp knife.

6 Make a well in the dry ingredients and pour in the egg mixture. With a spoon, stir until just blended. Add the apples, cranberries and walnuts and stir to blend.

7 Fill the muffin cups three-quarters full and bake for 25–30 minutes, or until well risen and firm in the middle. Transfer the muffins to a rack to cool. Dust lightly with icing sugar before serving, if desired.

Makes 12

60ml/4 tbsp butter or margarine
1 egg
175g/6oz/½ cup granulated sugar
grated rind of 1 large orange
120ml/4fl oz/½ cup fresh orange juice
175g/6oz/½ cup plain flour
2.5ml/½ tsp baking powder
2.5ml/½ tsp bicarbonate of soda
5ml/1 tsp ground cinnamon
2.5ml /½ tsp grated nutmeg
2.5ml/½ tsp ground allspice
1.25ml/¼ tsp ginger
1.25ml/¼ tsp salt
1–2 eating apples
115g/4oz/1 cup cranberries
50g/2oz/½ cup walnuts, chopped
icing sugar, for dusting (optional)

NUTRITION NOTES

Per portion	
Energy	175Kcals/733kJ
Fat	9.1g
Saturated Fat	1.4g
Cholesterol	16mg
Fibre	1.4g

Raspberry Muffins

These American muffins are made using baking powder and low fat buttermilk, giving them a light and spongy texture. They are delicious to eat at any time of the day.

Makes 10–12
275g/10oz/2½ cups plain flour
15ml/1 tbsp baking powder
115g/4oz/½ cup caster sugar
1 egg
250ml/8fl oz/1 cup buttermilk
60ml/4 tbsp sunflower oil
150g/5oz raspberries

NUTRITION NOTES
Per portion
Energy	171Kcals/719kJ
Fat	4.55g
Saturated Fat	0.71g
Cholesterol	16.5mg
Fibre	1.02g

1 Preheat the oven to 200°C/400°F/ Gas 6. Grease a 12-cup muffin tin or use paper liners. Sift the flour and baking powder into a mixing bowl, stir in the sugar, then make a well in the centre.

2 Mix the egg, buttermilk and sun- flower oil together in a bowl, pour into the flour mixture and mix quickly.

3 Add the raspberries and lightly fold in with a metal spoon. Spoon the mixture into the tin or paper cases.

4 Bake the muffins for 20–25 minutes until golden brown and firm in the middle. Transfer to a wire rack and serve warm or cold.

Spiced Banana Muffins

These light and nutritious muffins include banana for added fibre, and make a tasty tea-time treat.
If liked, slice off the tops and fill with jam.

Makes 12

75g/3oz/¾ cup plain wholemeal flour
50g/2oz/½ cup plain white flour
10ml/2 tsp baking powder
pinch of salt
5ml/1 tsp mixed spice
40g/1½oz/¼ cup soft light brown sugar
50g/2oz/¼ cup polyunsaturated
margarine
1 egg, beaten
150ml/¼ pint/⅔ cup semi-skimmed milk
grated rind of 1 orange
1 ripe banana
20g/¾oz/¼ cup porridge oats
20g/¾oz/scant ¼ cup chopped
hazelnuts

1 Preheat the oven to 200°C/400°F/ Gas 6. Grease a 12-cup muffin tin or use paper liners. Sift together both flours, the baking powder, salt and mixed spice into a bowl, then tip the bran remaining in the sieve into the bowl. Stir in the sugar.

2 Melt the margarine and pour it into a mixing bowl. Cool slightly, then beat in the egg, milk and grated orange rind.

4 Spoon the mixture into the tin or paper cases. Combine the oats and hazelnuts and sprinkle a little of the mixture over each muffin.

5 Bake in the preheated oven for 20 minutes until the muffins are well risen and golden, and a skewer inserted in the centre comes out clean. Transfer to a wire rack and allow to cool. These muffins can be served warm or cold.

NUTRITION NOTES

Per portion
Energy	139Kcals/582kJ
Fat	0.08g
Saturated Fat	0.1g
Cholesterol	0
Fibre	0.13g

3 Gently fold in the dry ingredients. Mash the banana with a fork, then stir it gently into the mixture, being careful not to overmix.

Carrot Muffins

Moist and full of flavour, these unusual muffins are a must.

Makes 12

175g/6oz/¾ cup margarine, at
room temperature
75g/3oz/½ cup dark brown sugar,
firmly packed
1 egg, at room temperature
15ml/1 tbsp water
150g/5oz/2 cups grated carrots
150g/5oz/1¼ cups plain flour
5ml/1 tsp baking powder
2.5ml/½ tsp bicarbonate of soda
5ml/1 tsp ground cinnamon
1.25ml/¼ tsp grated nutmeg
2.5ml/½ tsp salt

NUTRITION NOTES

Per portion
Energy   155Kcals/647kJ
Fat   9.2g
Saturated Fat   1.8g
Cholesterol   13mg
Fibre   0.8g

1 Preheat the oven to 180°C/350°F/ Gas 4. Grease a 12-cup muffin tin or use paper liners.

2 With an electric mixer, cream the margarine and sugar until they are light and fluffy. Beat in the egg and water. Stir in the carrots.

3 Sift over the flour, baking powder, bicarbonate of soda, cinnamon, nutmeg and salt. Stir to blend.

4 Spoon the batter into the prepared muffin cups, filling them almost to the top. Bake for about 35 minutes, until well risen and firm in the middle. Leave to stand for 10 minutes before transferring to a rack.

Dried Cherry Muffins

Muffins make a wonderful breakfast, particularly on special occasions.

1 In a mixing bowl, combine the yogurt and cherries. Cover and let stand for 30 minutes. Preheat the oven to 180°C/350°F/Gas 4. Grease 16 muffin cups or use paper liners.

2 With an electric mixer, cream the butter and sugar together until they are light and fluffy.

3 Add the eggs, one at a time, beating well after each addition.

4 Add the vanilla essence and the cherry mixture and stir to blend. Set aside. In another bowl, sift together the flour, baking powder, bicarbonate of soda and salt. Fold into the cherry mixture in three batches; do not overmix.

5 Fill the prepared muffin cups two-thirds full. For even baking, half-fill any empty cups with water. Bake for about 20 minutes, or until well risen and firm in the middle. Transfer to a rack.

Makes 16

225g/8oz/1 cup plain yogurt
225g/8oz/1 cup dried cherries
115g/4oz/½ cup butter, at room temperature
175g/6oz/¾ cup sugar
2 eggs, at room temperature
5ml/1 tsp vanilla essence
200g/7oz/1¾ cups plain flour
30ml/2 tsp baking powder
5ml/1 tsp bicarbonate of soda
0.75ml/⅛ tsp salt

NUTRITION NOTES

Per portion

Energy	197Kcals/826kJ
Fat	6.8g
Saturated Fat	1.4g
Cholesterol	25mg
Fibre	0.7g

Oatmeal Buttermilk Muffins

Add a Scottish flavour to your tea-time table.

Makes 12

75g/3oz/1 cup rolled oats
250ml/8fl oz/1 cup buttermilk
115g/4oz/8 tbsp butter, at
room temperature
75g/3oz/½ cup dark brown sugar,
firmly packed
1 egg, at room temperature
115g/4oz/1 cup plain flour
5ml/1 tsp baking powder
2.5ml/½ tsp salt
25g/1oz/¼ cup raisins

NUTRITION NOTES

Per portion

Energy	213Kcals/893kJ
Fat	9.3g
Saturated Fat	1.9g
Cholesterol	17mg
Fibre	1.2g

1 In a bowl, combine the oats and buttermilk and allow to soak for 1 hour.

2 Grease a 12-cup muffin tin or use paper liners.

3 Preheat the oven to 200°C/400°F/ Gas 6. With an electric mixer, cream the butter and sugar until light and fluffy. Beat in the egg.

4 In another bowl, sift together the flour, baking powder and salt. Stir the dry ingredients into the butter mixture, alternating with the oat mixture. Fold in the raisins, taking care not to overmix.

5 Fill the prepared cups two-thirds full. Bake for about 20–25 minutes, until a cake tester or skewer inserted in the centre comes out clean. Transfer to a wire rack to cool.

Pumpkin Muffins

Pumpkin has a mild, sweet flavour and makes a delicious, moist muffin.

1 Preheat the oven to 200°C/400°F/ Gas 6. Grease 14 muffin cups or use paper liners. With an electric mixer, cream the butter or margarine until soft. Add the sugar and molasses and beat until light and fluffy.

2 Add the egg and pumpkin and stir until well blended. Sift over the flour, salt, bicarbonate of soda, cinnamon and nutmeg. Fold just enough to blend; do not overmix.

3 Fold in the currants or raisins. Spoon the batter into the prepared muffin cups, filling them three-quarters full.

4 Bake for about 12–15 minutes, until well risen and firm in the middle. Transfer to a rack. Serve warm or cold.

Makes 14

115g/4oz/8 tbsp butter or margarine, at room temperature
⅔ cup dark brown sugar, firmly packed
150ml/¼ pint/⅔ cup molasses
1 egg, at room temperature, beaten
225g/8oz/1 cup cooked or canned pumpkin
200g/7oz/1¾ cups plain flour
1.25ml/¼ tsp salt
5ml/1 tsp bicarbonate of soda
7.5ml/1½ tsp ground cinnamon
5ml/1 tsp grated nutmeg
25g/1oz/¼ cup currants or raisins

NUTRITION NOTES
Per portion

Energy	196Kcals/821kJ
Fat	7.3g
Saturated Fat	1.4g
Cholesterol	14mg
Fibre	0.8g

Raisin Bran Muffins

High in fibre and high in flavour, a real treat.

Makes 15

60ml/4 tbsp butter or margarine
75g/3oz/¾ cup all-purpose flour
50g/2oz/½ cup wholewheat flour
7.5ml/1½ tsp bicarbonate of soda
0.75ml/⅛ tsp salt
5ml/1 tsp ground cinnamon
40g/1½oz/½ cup bran
75g/3oz/½ cup raisins
50g/2oz/⅓ cup dark brown sugar,
firmly packed
50g/2oz/¼ cup granulated sugar
1 egg
250ml/8fl oz/1 cup buttermilk
juice of ½ lemon

1 Preheat the oven to 200°C/400°F/ Gas 6. Grease 15 muffin cups or use paper liners.

2 Place the butter or margarine in a heavy-based saucepan and melt over a gentle heat.

3 In a mixing bowl, sift together the all-purpose flour, wholewheat flour, bicarbonate of soda, salt and cinnamon.

4 Add the bran, raisins and sugars and stir until blended.

5 In another bowl, mix together the egg, buttermilk, lemon juice and melted butter.

6 Add the buttermilk mixture to the dry ingredients. Stir lightly and quickly just until moistened; do not mix until smooth as this will ruin the texture.

7 Spoon the batter into the prepared muffin cups, filling them almost to the top. Half-fill any empty cups with water before placing in the oven.

8 Bake until golden, for 15–20 minutes. Serve at room temperature.

NUTRITION NOTES

Per portion
Energy	131Kcals/551kJ
Fat	4.1g
Saturated Fat	0.9g
Cholesterol	13mg
Fibre	1.7g

Prune Muffins

All sorts of fruit can be used to make a delicious filling for muffins – prunes are a healthy alternative.

Makes 12
1 egg
250ml/8fl oz/1 cup skimmed milk
50ml/2fl oz/¼ cup vegetable oil
50g/2oz/¼ cup granulated sugar
30ml/2 tbsp dark brown sugar
225g/8oz/2 cups plain flour
30ml/2 tsp baking powder
2.5ml/½ tsp salt
1.25ml/¼ tsp grated nutmeg
150g/5oz/¾ cup cooked pitted
prunes, chopped

NUTRITION NOTES
Per portion
Energy	177Kcals/745kJ
Fat	4.6g
Saturated Fat	0.6g
Cholesterol	16mg
Fibre	1.5g

1 Preheat the oven to 200°C/400°F/ Gas 6. Grease a 12-cup muffin tin or use paper liners.

2 Break the egg into a mixing bowl and beat with a fork. Beat in the milk and oil. Stir in the sugars. Set aside.

3 Sift the flour, baking powder, salt and nutmeg into a mixing bowl. Make a well in the centre, pour in the egg mixture and stir until moistened. Do not overmix; the batter should be slightly lumpy.

4 Fold in the prunes.

5 Fill the prepared cups two-thirds full. Bake until golden brown, about 20 minutes. Let stand for 10 minutes before unmoulding. Serve warm or at room temperature.

Yogurt Honey Muffins

Serve with low fat Greek yogurt and a drizzle of honey for a delicious treat.

1 Preheat the oven to 190°C/375°F/ Gas 5. Grease a 12-cup muffin tin or use paper liners.

2 In a saucepan, melt the butter and honey. Remove from the heat and set aside to cool slightly.

3 In a bowl, whisk together the yogurt, egg, lemon rind and juice.

4 In another bowl, sift together the dry ingredients.

5 Fold the dry ingredients into the yogurt mixture just to blend.

6 Fill the prepared cups two-thirds full. Bake for 20–25 minutes, until well risen and firm in the middle. Let cool in the tin for 5 minutes before unmoulding. Serve warm or at room temperature.

Makes 12

60ml/4 tbsp butter
75ml/5 tbsp thin honey
225g/8oz/1 cup plain yogurt
1 large egg, at room temperature
grated rind of 1 lemon
150ml/2fl oz/¼ cup fresh lemon juice
115g/4oz/1 cup all-purpose flour
115g/4oz/1 cup wholewheat flour
7.5ml/1½ tsp bicarbonate of soda
0.75ml/⅛ tsp grated nutmeg

NUTRITION NOTES
Per portion

Energy	131Kcals/551kJ
Fat	4.1g
Saturated Fat	0.9g
Cholesterol	13mg
Fibre	1.7g

Variation

For Walnut Yogurt Honey Muffins, add 50g/2oz/½ cup chopped walnuts, folding in with the flour. This makes a more substantial muffin.

Blackberry, Sloe Gin and Rosewater Muffins

Bring a taste of the countryside to tea time with tantalising hedgerow fruits and delicate rosewater.

Makes 12

300g/11oz/2½ cups plain white flour
50g/2oz/generous ¼ cup light brown sugar
60ml/4 tsp baking powder
pinch of salt
60g/2¼oz/generous 1 cup chopped blanched almonds
90g/3½oz/generous ½ cup fresh blackberries
2 eggs
200ml/7fl oz/⅞ cup milk
60ml/4 tbsp melted butter
15ml/1 tbsp sloe gin
15ml/1 tbsp rosewater

NUTRITION NOTES

Per portion
Energy	194Kcals/813kJ
Fat	8.1g
Saturated Fat	1.32g
Cholesterol	32.8mg
Fibre	1.4g

1 Preheat the oven to 200°C/400°F/ Gas 6. Grease a 12-cup muffin tin or use paper liners. Mix the flour, sugar, baking powder and salt in a bowl and stir in the almonds and blackberries, mixing them well to coat with the flour mixture.

2 In another bowl, mix the eggs with the milk, then gradually add the butter, sloe gin and rosewater. Make a well in the centre of the bowl of dry ingredients and add the egg and milk mixture. Stir well.

3 Spoon the mixture into the greased muffin tin or cases. Bake for 20–25 minutes or until browned. Turn out the muffins on to a wire rack to cool. Serve with butter.

Date and Apple Muffins

You will only need one or two of these wholesome muffins per person, as they are very filling.

1 Preheat the oven to 200°C/400°F/ Gas 6. Grease a 12-cup muffin tin or use paper liners. Put the wholemeal flour in a mixing bowl. Sift in the white flour with the cinnamon and baking powder. Rub in the margarine until the mixture resembles breadcrumbs, then stir in the muscovado sugar.

2 Quarter and core the apple, chop the flesh finely and set aside. Stir a little of the apple juice with the pear and apple spread until smooth. Mix in the remaining juice, then add to the rubbed-in dry ingredients with the egg. Add the chopped apple to the bowl with the dates. Mix quickly until just combined.

3 Divide the mixture evenly among the muffin cases.

4 Sprinkle with the chopped pecan nuts. Bake the muffins for 20–25 minutes until golden brown and firm in the middle. Transfer to a wire rack and serve while still warm.

Cook's Tip

Use a pear in place of the eating apple and chopped ready-to-eat dried apricots in place of the dates. Ground mixed spice is a good alternative to cinnamon.

Makes 12

150g/5oz/1¼ cups self-raising wholemeal flour
150g/5oz/1¼ cups self-raising white flour
5ml/1 tsp ground cinnamon
5ml/1 tsp baking powder
25g/1oz/2 tbsp soft margarine
75g/3oz/½ cup light muscovado sugar
1 eating apple
250ml/8fl oz/1 cup apple juice
30ml/2 tbsp pear and apple spread
1 egg, lightly beaten
75g/3oz/½ cup chopped dates
15ml/1 tbsp chopped pecan nuts

NUTRITION NOTES
Per portion

Energy	163Kcals/686kJ
Fat	2.98g
Saturated Fat	0.47g
Cholesterol	16.04mg
Fibre	1.97g

Cherry Marmalade Muffins

Serve with marmalade for a tasty breakfast.

Makes 12

225g/8oz/2 cups self-raising flour
5ml/1 tsp ground mixed spice
75g/3oz/6 tbsp caster sugar
115g/4oz/½ cup glacé
cherries, quartered
30ml/2 tbsp orange marmalade
150ml/¼ pint/½ cup skimmed milk
50g/2oz/4 tbsp soft
sunflower margarine
marmalade, to brush

NUTRITION NOTES

Per portion
Energy	154Kcals/650kJ
Fat	3.66g
Saturated Fat	0.68g
Cholesterol	0.54mg
Fibre	0.69g

1 Preheat the oven to 200°C/400°F/ Gas 6. Lightly grease a 12-cup muffin tin or use paper liners.

2 Sift together the flour and spice, then stir in the sugar and cherries.

3 Mix the marmalade with the milk and beat into the dry ingredients with the margarine. Spoon in to the greased tins. Bake for 20–25 minutes, until golden brown and firm in the middle.

4 Turn out on to a wire rack and brush the tops with warmed marmalade. Serve warm or cold.

Fruit Salad Slices

Try these delicious fruit salad slices as an alternative to a traditional fruit cake.

1 Soak the dried fruits in the tea for several hours, or overnight. Drain and reserve the liquid.

2 Preheat the oven to 180°C/350°F/ Gas 4. Grease an 18cm/7in round cake tin and line the base with non-stick baking paper.

3 Sift the flour into a bowl with the nutmeg. Stir in the muscovado sugar, fruit and tea. Add the oil and milk and mix well.

4 Spoon the mixture into the prepared tin and sprinkle with demerara sugar. Bake for 50–55 minutes or until firm. Turn out and cool on a wire rack.

Serves 8

175g/6oz/¼ cup roughly chopped dried fruit salad mixture, e.g. apples, apricots, prunes and peaches
250ml/8fl oz/1 cup hot black tea
225g/8oz/2 cups wholemeal self-raising flour
5ml/1 tsp grated nutmeg
50g/2oz/4 tbsp dark muscovado sugar
45ml/3 tbsp sunflower oil
45ml/3 tbsp skimmed milk
demerara sugar, to sprinkle

NUTRITION NOTES

Per portion
Energy	201Kcals/848kJ
Fat	4.99g
Saturated Fat	0.65g
Cholesterol	0.1mg
Fibre	3.89g

Pineapple and Cinnamon Drop Scones

Making the batter with pineapple juice instead of milk cuts down on fat and adds to the taste.

Makes 24

115g/4oz/1 cup self-raising
wholemeal flour
115g/4oz/1 cup self-raising white flour
5ml/1 tsp ground cinnamon
15ml/1 tbsp caster sugar
1 egg, beaten
300ml/½ pint/1¼ cups pineapple juice
75g/3oz/½ cup semi-dried
pineapple, chopped

NUTRITION NOTES

Per portion

Energy	51Kcals/215kJ
Fat	0.81g
Saturated Fat	0.14g
Cholesterol	8.02mg
Fibre	0.76g

2 Add the egg with half the pineapple juice and gradually incorporate the surrounding flour to make a smooth batter. Beat in the remaining juice with the chopped pineapple.

1 Preheat a griddle, heavy-based frying pan or an electric frying pan. Put the wholemeal flour in a mixing bowl. Sift in the white flour, add the cinnamon and sugar and make a well in the centre.

3 Lightly grease the griddle or pan. Drop tablespoons of the batter on to the surface, leaving them until they bubble and the bubbles begin to burst.

4 Turn the drop scones with a palette knife and cook until the underside is golden brown. Keep the cooked scones warm and moist by wrapping them in a clean napkin while continuing to cook successive batches.

Drop Scones

These little scones are delicious spread with jam.

1 Preheat a griddle, heavy-based frying pan or an electric frying pan. Sift the flour and salt into a mixing bowl. Stir in the sugar and make a well in the centre.

2 Add the egg and half the milk, then gradually incorporate the surrounding flour to make a smooth batter. Beat in the remaining milk.

3 Lightly oil the griddle or pan. Drop tablespoons of the batter on to the surface, leaving them until they bubble and the bubbles begin to burst.

4 Turn the drop scones over with a palette knife and cook until the underside is golden brown. Keep the cooked drop scones warm and moist by wrapping them in a clean napkin while cooking successive batches.

Makes 18

225g/8oz/2 cups self-raising flour
2.5ml/½ tsp salt
15ml/1 tbsp caster sugar
1 egg, beaten
300ml/½ pint/1¼ cups skimmed milk
oil, for frying

NUTRITION NOTES

Per portion

Energy	64Kcals/270kJ
Fat	1.09g
Saturated Fat	0.2g
Cholesterol	11.04mg
Fibre	0.43g

Cook's Tip

For savoury scones, add 2 chopped spring onions and 15ml/1 tbsp freshly grated Parmesan cheese. Serve with cottage cheese.

Wholewheat Scones

Made with a mixture of flours, these scones are a high fibre, healthy alternative.

Makes 16

175g/6oz/¾ cup cold butter
225g/8oz/2 cups wholewheat flour
175g/6oz/1 cup all-purpose flour
30ml/2 tbsp sugar
2.5ml/½ tsp salt
12.5ml/2½ tsp bicarbonate of soda
2 eggs
175ml/6fl oz/¾ cup buttermilk
25g/1oz/¼ cup raisins

NUTRITION NOTES

Per portion
Energy   197Kcals/826kJ
Fat   9.8g
Saturated Fat   2g
Cholesterol   25mg
Fibre   2g

1 Preheat the oven to 200°C/400°F/ Gas 6. Grease and flour a large baking sheet.

2 Cut the butter into small pieces with a blunt knife.

3 Combine the dry ingredients in a bowl. Add the butter and cut in with a pastry blender until the mixture resembles coarse crumbs. Set aside.

4 In another bowl, whisk together the eggs and buttermilk. Set aside 30ml/2 tbsp for glazing.

5 Stir the remaining egg mixture into the dry ingredients until it just holds together. Stir in the raisins.

6 Roll out the dough about 2cm/¾in thick. Stamp out rounds with a cutter. Place on the prepared sheet and brush with the reserved glaze.

7 Bake in the preheated oven for 12–15 minutes, until golden. Allow to cool slightly before serving.

Orange Raisin Scones

A tang of orange gives these scones a special flavour.

1 Preheat the oven to 220°C/425°F/ Gas 7. Grease and flour a large baking sheet.

2 Combine the dry ingredients in a large bowl. Add the butter and margarine and cut in with a pastry blender until the mixture resembles coarse crumbs.

3 Add the orange rind and raisins. Gradually stir in the buttermilk to form a soft dough.

4 Roll out the dough about 2cm/¾in thick. Stamp out rounds with a cutter.

5 Place on the prepared sheet and brush the tops with milk. Bake for about 12–15 minutes, until golden. Serve hot or warm.

Makes 16

225g/8oz/2 cups flour
25ml/1½ tbsp baking powder
75g/3oz/⅓ cup sugar
2.5ml/½ tsp salt
75ml/5 tbsp butter, diced
75ml/5 tbsp margarine, diced
grated rind of 1 large orange
50g/2oz/⅓ cup raisins
115g/4oz/½ cup buttermilk
milk, for glazing

NUTRITION NOTES

Per portion
Energy   164Kcals/687kJ
Fat   7.9g
Saturated Fat   1.6g
Cholesterol   1mg
Fibre   0.7g

Cook's Tip

For light tender scones, handle the dough as little as possible. If you wish, split the scones when cool and toast them under a preheated grill. Butter them while still hot.

Sunflower Sultana Scones

Add a bit of crunch to your scones with this combination of sunflower seeds and sultanas.

Makes 10–12

225g/8oz/2 cups self-raising flour
5ml/1 tsp baking powder
25g/1oz/2 tbsp soft sunflower margarine
25g/1oz/2 tbsp golden caster sugar
50g/2oz/⅓ cup sultanas
30ml/2 tbsp sunflower seeds
150g/5oz/⅔ cup natural yogurt
about 30–45ml/2–3 tbsp skimmed milk

NUTRITION NOTES

Per portion

Energy	176Kcals/742kJ
Fat	5.32g
SaturatedFat	0.81g
Cholesterol	0.84mg
Fibre	1.26g

1 Preheat the oven to 230°C/450°F/ Gas 8. Lightly oil a baking sheet. Sift the flour and baking powder into a bowl and rub in the margarine evenly.

2 Stir in the sugar, sultanas and half the sunflower seeds, then mix in the yogurt, with just enough milk to make a fairly soft, but not sticky dough.

3 Roll out on a lightly floured surface to about 2cm/¾in thickness. Cut into 6cm/2½in flower shapes or rounds with a biscuit cutter and lift on to the baking sheet.

4 Brush with milk and sprinkle with the reserved sunflower seeds, then bake for 10–12 minutes, until well risen and golden brown.

5 Cool the scones on a wire rack. Serve split and spread with jam or low fat spread.

Prune and Peel Rock Buns

Split these buns and serve with fromage frais, if wished.

Makes 12

225g/8oz/2 cups plain flour
10ml/2 tsp baking powder
75g/3oz/⅔ cup demerara sugar
50g/2oz/½ cup chopped ready-to-eat dried prunes
50g/2oz/⅓ cup chopped mixed peel
finely grated rind of 1 lemon
50ml/2fl oz/¼ cup sunflower oil
75ml/5 tbsp skimmed milk

1 Preheat the oven to 200°C/400°F/ Gas 6. Lightly oil a large baking sheet. Sift together the flour and baking powder, then stir in the sugar, prunes, peel and lemon rind.

2 Mix the oil and milk, then stir into the mixture, to make a dough that just binds together.

3 Spoon into rocky heaps on the baking sheet and bake for 20 minutes, until golden. Cool on a wire rack.

NUTRITION NOTES

Per portion

Energy	135Kcals/570kJ
Fat	3.35g
Saturated Fat	0.44g
Cholesterol	0.13mg
Fibre	0.86g

Banana and Apricot Chelsea Buns

These buns are old favourites given a low fat twist with a delectable fruit filling.

Serves 9

90ml/6 tbsp warm skimmed milk
5ml/1 tsp dried yeast
pinch of sugar
225g/8oz/2 cups strong plain flour
10ml/2 tsp mixed spice
2.5ml/½ tsp salt
50g/2oz/¼ cup caster sugar
25g/1oz/2 tbsp soft margarine
1 egg

For the filling

1 large ripe banana
175g/6oz/1 cup ready-to-eat
dried apricots
30ml/2 tbsp caster sugar
30ml/2 tbsp light muscovado sugar

For the glaze

30ml/2 tbsp caster sugar
30ml/2 tbsp water

Cook's Tip

Do not leave the buns in the tin for too long or the glaze will stick to the sides, making them very difficult to remove.

NUTRITION NOTES

Per portion
Energy	214Kcals/901kJ
Fat	2.18g
Saturated Fat	0.63g
Cholesterol	21.59mg
Fibre	2.18g

1 Lightly grease an 18cm/7in square tin. Put the warm milk in a jug and sprinkle the yeast on top. Add a pinch of sugar to help activate the yeast, mix well and leave for 30 minutes.

2 Sift the flour, spice and salt into a mixing bowl. Stir in the caster sugar, rub in the margarine, then stir in the yeast mixture and the egg. Gradually mix in the flour to make a soft dough, adding extra milk if needed.

3 Turn out the dough on to a floured surface and knead for 5 minutes until smooth and elastic. Return the dough to the clean bowl, cover with a damp tea towel and leave in a warm place for about 2 hours, until doubled in bulk.

4 To prepare the filling, mash the banana in a bowl. Using scissors, snip the apricots into pieces, then stir into the banana with the sugars.

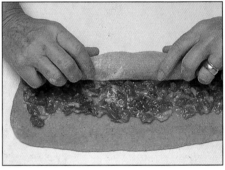

5 Knead the dough on a floured surface for 2 minutes, then roll out to a 30 x 23cm/12 x 9in rectangle. Spread the banana and apricot filling over the dough and roll up lengthways like a Swiss roll, with the join underneath.

6 Cut the roll into 9 buns. Place, cut side down, in the tin, cover and leave to rise for 30 minutes. Preheat the oven to 200°C/400°F/Gas 6 and bake for 20–25 minutes. Meanwhile, mix the caster sugar and water in a small saucepan. Heat, stirring, until dissolved, then boil for 2 minutes. Brush the glaze over the cooked buns while still hot.

Blueberry Streusel Slice

This soft berry filling tastes delicious with the nutty topping.

Makes about 30 slices

225g/8oz ready-prepared shortcrust pastry
50g/2oz/½ cup plain flour
1.25ml/¼ tsp baking powder
40g/1½oz/3 tbsp butter or margarine
50g/2oz/⅓ cup soft light brown sugar
25g/1oz/2 tbsp fresh
white breadcrumbs
1.5ml/¼ tsp salt
50g/2oz/4 tbsp flaked or chopped almonds
30ml/4 tbsp blackberry or bramble jelly
115g/4oz blueberries, fresh or frozen

NUTRITION NOTES

Per portion

Energy	77Kcals/322kJ
Fat	4.16g
Saturated Fat	1.57g
Cholesterol	5.84mg
Fibre	0.95g

1 Preheat the oven to 180°F/350°F/ Gas 4. Roll out the pastry on a lightly floured surface to line an 18 x 28cm/ 7 x 11in Swiss roll tin. Prick the base evenly with a fork.

2 Rub together the flour, baking powder, butter or margarine, sugar, breadcrumbs and salt until really crumbly, then mix in the almonds.

3 Spread the pastry with the jelly, sprinkle with the blueberries, then cover evenly with the streusel topping, pressing down lightly. Bake for 20 minutes, then reduce the temperature to 170°C/325°F/Gas 3 and cook for a further 10–20 minutes.

4 Remove from the oven when golden on the top and the pastry is cooked through. Cut into slices while still hot, then allow to cool.

Sticky Date and Apple Bars

If possible, allow this mixture to mature for 1–2 days before cutting – it will get stickier and better!

1 Preheat the oven to 190°C/375°F/ Gas 5. Line an 18–20cm/7–8in square or rectangular loose-based cake tin. In a large pan, heat the margarine, sugar, syrup and dates, stirring until the dates soften completely.

2 Gradually work in the oats, flour, apples and lemon juice until well mixed. Spoon into the tin and spread out evenly. Top with the walnut halves.

3 Bake for 30 minutes, then reduce the temperature to 170°C/325°F/Gas 3 and bake for 10–20 minutes more, until firm to the touch and golden. Cut into squares or bars while still warm, and keep for 1–2 days before eating.

Makes about 16 bars

115g/4oz/½ cup margarine
50g/2oz/4 tbsp soft dark brown sugar
50g/2oz/4 tbsp golden syrup
115g/4oz/¾ cup chopped dates
115g/4oz/1/¼ cups rolled oats
115g/4oz/1 cup wholemeal
self-raising flour
225g/8oz/2 eating apples, peeled,
cored and grated
5–10ml/1–2 tsp lemon juice
20–25 walnut halves

NUTRITION NOTES

Per portion

Energy	183Kcals/763kJ
Fat	10.11g
Saturated Fat	1.64g
Cholesterol	0.14mg
Fibre	1g

Apricot Sponge Bars

These fingers are delicious at tea time – the apricots keep them moist for several days.

Makes 18

225g/8oz/2 cups self-raising flour
115g/4oz/½ cup soft light brown sugar
50g/2oz/½ cup semolina
175g/6oz/1 cup ready-to-eat dried
apricots, chopped
30ml/2 tbsp clear honey
30ml/2 tbsp malt extract
2 eggs
60ml/4 tbsp skimmed milk
60ml/4 tbsp sunflower oil
a few drops of almond essence
30ml/2 tbsp flaked almonds

NUTRITION NOTES

Per portion
Energy   153Kcals/641kJ
Fat   4.5g
Saturated Fat   0.61g
Cholesterol   21.5mg
Fibre   1.27g

1 Preheat the oven to 160°C/325°F/ Gas 3. Lightly grease and then line an 18 x 28cm/7 x 11in baking tin.

2 Sift the flour into a bowl and mix in the sugar, semolina and apricots. Make a well in the centre and add the honey, malt extract, eggs, milk, oil and almond essence. Mix the ingredients together thoroughly until smooth.

3 Spoon the mixture into the tin, spreading it to the edges, then sprinkle over the flaked almonds.

4 Bake for 30–35 minutes, or until the centre springs back when lightly pressed. Remove from the tin and turn on to a wire rack to cool. Cut into 18 slices using a sharp knife.

Cook's Tip

If you can't find pre-soaked apricots, use chopped ordinary dried apricots soaked in boiling water for 1 hour, then drain and add to the mixture.

Apricot Yogurt Cookies

These soft cookies are very quick to make and are useful for lunch boxes.

1 Preheat the oven to 190°C/375°F/ Gas 5. Lightly oil a large baking sheet.

2 Sift together the flour, baking powder and cinnamon. Stir in the oats, sugar, apricots and nuts.

3 Beat together the yogurt and oil, then stir evenly into the mixture to make a firm dough. If necessary, add a little more yogurt.

4 Use your hands to roll the mixture into about 16 small balls, place on the baking sheet and flatten with a fork.

5 Sprinkle with demerara sugar. Bake for 15–20 minutes, or until firm and golden brown. Leave to cool on a wire rack.

Makes 16

175g/6oz/1½ cups plain flour
5ml/1 tsp baking powder
5ml/1 tsp ground cinnamon
75g/3oz/1 cup rolled oats
75g/3oz/½ cup light muscovado sugar
115g/4oz/½ cup chopped ready-to-eat dried apricots
15ml/1 tbsp flaked hazelnuts or almonds
150g/5oz/⅔ cup natural yogurt
45ml/3 tbsp sunflower oil
demerara sugar, to sprinkle

NUTRITION NOTES

Per portion

Energy	95Kcals/400kJ
Fat	2.66g
Saturated Fat	0.37g
Cholesterol	0.3mg
Fibre	0.94g

Cook's Tip

These cookies do not keep well, so it is best to eat them within two days, or to freeze them. Pack into polythene bags and freeze for up to four months.

Buttermilk Biscuits

Low in fat, these biscuits are perfect for a mid-morning snack.

Makes 15

75g/6oz/1½ cups plain flour
5ml/1 tsp salt
5ml/1 tsp baking powder
2.5ml/½ tsp bicarbonate of soda
60ml/4 tbsp cold butter or margarine
175ml/6fl oz/¾ cup buttermilk

NUTRITION NOTES

Per portion
Energy	85Kcals/359kJ
Fat	3.5g
Saturated Fat	0.7g
Cholesterol	0.5mg
Fibre	0.5g

1 Preheat the oven to 220°C/425°F/ Gas 7. Grease a baking sheet. Sift the dry ingredients into a bowl. Cut in the butter or margarine with a pastry blender until the mixture resembles coarse crumbs.

2 Gradually pour in the buttermilk, stirring with a fork to form a soft dough.

3 Roll out the biscuit dough to about a 1cm/½in thickness.

4 Stamp out 5cm/2in rounds with a biscuit cutter. Place on the prepared tray and bake for 12–15 minutes, or until golden. Serve warm or at room temperature.

Shortcake

Delicious served warm with a low fat spread.

1 Preheat the oven to 220°C/425°F/ Gas 7. Grease a baking sheet.

2 Sift the flour, sugar, baking powder and salt into a bowl.

3 Cut in the butter with a pastry blender until the mixture resembles coarse crumbs.

4 Pour in the milk and stir with a fork to form a soft dough.

5 Roll out the dough to about 5mm/¼in thickness. Stamp out rounds with a 6cm/2½in biscuit cutter. Place on the prepared sheet and bake for about 12 minutes, or until golden. Serve hot or warm.

Makes 8

165g/5½oz/1⅓ cups plain flour
30ml/2 tbsp sugar
15ml/3 tsp baking powder
0.75ml/⅛ tsp salt
75ml/5 tbsp cold butter, cut in pieces
120ml/4fl oz/½ cup skimmed milk

NUTRITION NOTES
Per portion

Energy	176Kcals/740kJ
Fat	8g
Saturated Fat	1.5g
Cholesterol	1mg
Fibre	0.8g

Variation

For Berry Shortcake, split the biscuits in half while still warm. Top one half with lightly sugared fresh berries such as strawberries, raspberries or blueberries, and sandwich with the other half. Serve with dollops of thick, low fat yogurt.

Oaty Crisps

These biscuits are very crisp and crunchy – ideal to serve with morning coffee.

Makes 18

175g/6oz/1¾ cups rolled oats
75g/3oz/½ cup light muscovado sugar
1 egg
60ml/4 tbsp sunflower oil
30ml/2 tbsp malt extract

NUTRITION NOTES

Per portion

Energy	86Kcals/360kJ
Fat	3.59g
Saturated Fat	0.57g
Cholesterol	10.7mg
Fibre	0.66g

1 Preheat the oven to 190°C/375°F/ Gas 5. Lightly grease two baking sheets. Mix the rolled oats and sugar in a bowl, breaking up any lumps in the sugar. Add the egg, sunflower oil and malt extract, mix well, then leave to soak for 15 minutes.

2 Using a teaspoon, place small heaps of the mixture well apart on the prepared baking sheets. Press the heaps into 7.5cm/3in rounds with the back of a dampened fork.

3 Bake the biscuits for 10–15 minutes until golden brown. Leave them to cool for 1 minute, then remove with a palette knife and cool on a wire rack.

Cook's Tip

To give these biscuits a coarser texture, substitute jumbo oats for some or all of the rolled oats. Once cool, store the biscuits in an airtight container to keep them as crisp and fresh as possible.

Orange Cookies

A popular choice for a well-earned coffee break.

1 With an electric mixer, cream the butter and sugar until light and fluffy. Add the yolks, orange juice and rind, and continue beating to blend. Set aside.

2 In another bowl, sift together the flours, salt and baking powder. Add to the butter mixture and stir until it forms a dough.

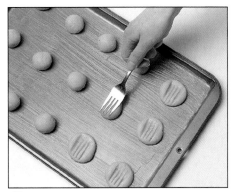

6 Press down with a fork to flatten. Bake for 8–10 minutes, until golden brown. With a metal spatula, transfer to a rack to cool.

Makes 30

115g/4oz/8 tbsp butter, at room temperature
200g/7oz/1 cup sugar
2 egg yolks
15ml/1 tbsp fresh orange juice
grated rind of 1 orange
175g/6oz/1 cup plain flour
115g/4oz/½ cup cake flour
2.5ml/½ tsp salt
5ml/1 tsp baking powder

NUTRITION NOTES

Per portion

Energy	84Kcals/353kJ
Fat	3.5g
Saturated Fat	0.7g
Cholesterol	14mg
Fibre	0.2g

3 Wrap the dough in greaseproof paper and chill for 2 hours.

4 Preheat the oven to 190°C/375°F/ Gas 5. Grease two baking sheets.

5 Roll spoonfuls of the dough into balls and place 2.5–5cm/1–2in apart on the prepared sheets.

Breads

The aroma of freshly-
baked bread makes
every house feel like a
home. And these low
fat loaves also taste
tantalizingly good.

White Bread

The classic white loaf, perfect for breakfast toast.

Makes 2 loaves

50ml/2fl oz/¼ cup lukewarm water
10ml/2 tsp active dry yeast
30ml/2 tbsp sugar
475ml/16fl oz/2 cups lukewarm skimmed milk
30ml/2 tbsp butter or margarine, at room temperature
10ml/2 tsp salt
675–825g/1½–1¾lb/6–6½ cups flour

NUTRITION NOTES

Per portion
Energy	178Kcals/757kJ
Fat	1.8g
Saturated Fat	0.3g
Cholesterol	1g
Fibre	1.4g

1 Combine the water, yeast and 1 table-spoon of sugar in a measuring cup and leave for 15 minutes.

2 Pour the milk into a large bowl. Add the remaining sugar, the butter or margarine, the salt and the yeast mixture.

3 Stir in the flour, 115g/4oz/1 cup at a time, until a stiff dough is obtained. Alternatively, use a food processor.

4 Transfer the dough to a floured surface. To knead, push the dough away from you with the palm of your hand, then fold it towards you, and push it away again. Repeat until the dough is smooth and elastic.

5 Place the dough in a large greased bowl, cover with a plastic bag, and leave to rise in a warm place until doubled in volume, 2–3 hours. Grease two 23 x 13cm/9 x 5in loaf tins.

6 Punch down the risen dough with your fist and divide in half. Form into loaf shapes and place in the tins, seam-side down. Cover and let rise in a warm place until almost doubled in volume, about 45 minutes.

7 Preheat the oven to 190°C/375°F/ Gas 5. Bake for 45–50 minutes, until firm and brown. Unmould and tap the bottom of a loaf: if it sounds hollow, the loaf is done. If necessary, return to the oven and bake a few minutes more. Transfer to a rack to cool.

Country Bread

A wholewheat loaf that is high in fibre and low in fat.

1 For the starter, combine the yeast, water, flour and sugar in a bowl and stir with a fork. Cover and leave in a warm place for 2–3 hours, or leave overnight in a cool place.

2 Place the flours, salt and butter in a food processor and process just until blended, for 1–2 minutes. Stir together the milk and starter, then slowly pour into the processor, with the motor running, until the mixture forms a dough. If necessary, add more water. Alternatively, the dough can be mixed by hand. Transfer to a floured surface and knead until smooth and elastic.

3 Place in an ungreased bowl, cover with a plastic bag, and leave to rise in a warm place until doubled in volume, for about 1½ hours. Transfer to a floured surface and knead briefly. Return to the bowl and leave to rise until tripled in volume, about 1½ hours.

4 Divide the dough in half. Cut off one-third of the dough from each half and shape into balls. Shape the larger remaining halves into balls. Grease a baking sheet.

5 For each loaf, top the large ball with the small ball and press the centre with the handle of a wooden spoon to secure. Cover with a plastic bag, slash the top, and leave to rise.

6 Preheat the oven to 200°C/400°F/ Gas 6. Dust the dough with wholewheat flour and bake for 45–50 minutes, until the top is browned and the bottom sounds hollow when tapped. Cool on a rack before serving.

Serves 12

275g/10oz/2½ cups wholewheat flour
275g/10oz/2½ cups plain flour
115g/4oz/1 cup strong white flour
20ml/4 tsp salt
60ml/4 tbsp butter, at room temperature
475ml/16fl oz/2 cups lukewarm milk

For the starter

10ml/2tsp active dry yeast
250ml/8fl oz/1 cup lukewarm water
115g/4oz/1 cup plain flour
1.5ml/¼ tsp sugar

NUTRITION NOTES

Per portion

Energy	204Kcals/863kJ
Fat	3.3g
Saturated Fat	0.6g
Cholesterol	1mg
Fibre	2.7g

Poppy Seed Rolls

Pile these soft rolls in a basket and serve them for breakfast or with dinner.

Makes 12
300ml/½ pint/1¼ cups warm skimmed milk
5ml/1 tsp dried yeast
pinch of sugar
450g/1lb/4 cups strong white flour
5ml/1 tsp salt
1 egg, lightly beaten

For the topping
1 egg, beaten
poppy seeds

Cook's Tip
Use easy-blend dried yeast if you prefer. Add it directly to the dry ingredients and mix with hand-hot milk. The rolls will only require one rising (see package instructions). Vary the toppings. Linseed, sesame seeds and caraway seeds are all good; try adding caraway seeds to the dough, too, for extra flavour.

NUTRITION NOTES
Per portion
Energy	160Kcals/674kJ
Fat	2.42g
Saturated Fat	0.46g
Cholesterol	32.58mg
Fibre	1.16g

1 Put half the warm milk in a small bowl. Sprinkle the yeast on top. Add the sugar, mix well and leave to stand for 30 minutes.

2 Sift the flour and salt into a mixing bowl. Make a well in the centre and pour in the yeast mixture and the egg. Gradually incorporate the flour, adding enough of the remaining milk to mix to a soft dough.

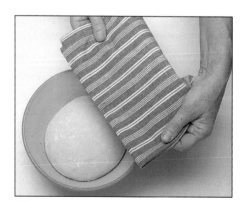

3 Turn the dough on to a floured surface and knead for 5 minutes until smooth and elastic. Return to the clean bowl, cover with a damp tea towel and leave in a warm place to rise for about 1 hour until doubled in bulk.

4 Lightly grease two baking sheets. Turn the dough on to a floured surface. Knead for 2 minutes, then cut into 12 pieces and shape into rolls.

5 Place the rolls on the prepared baking sheets, cover loosely with a large plastic bag (ballooning it to trap the air inside) and leave to stand in a warm place until the rolls have risen well. Preheat the oven to 220°C/425°F/Gas 7.

6 Glaze the rolls with the beaten egg, sprinkle with poppy seeds and bake for 12–15 minutes until golden brown. Transfer to a wire rack to cool.

Braided Loaf

An attractive, traditional loaf that would be fun as a dinner party accompaniment.

Serves 10

10ml/2 tsp active dry yeast
5ml/1 tsp honey
250ml/8fl oz/1 cup lukewarm
skimmed milk
60ml/4 tbsp butter, melted
350g/12oz/3 cups flour
5ml/1 tsp salt
1 egg, lightly beaten
1 egg yolk, beaten with 5ml/1 tsp
skimmed milk, for glazing

NUTRITION NOTES

Per portion
Energy	222Kcals/938kJ
Fat	6.6g
Saturated Fat	1.35g
Cholesterol	40.3mg
Fibre	1.4g

1 Combine the yeast, honey, milk and butter, stir, and leave for 15 minutes to dissolve.

2 In a large bowl, mix together the flour and salt. Make a well in the centre and add the yeast mixture and egg. With a wooden spoon, stir from the centre, incorporating flour with each turn, to obtain a rough dough.

3 Transfer to a floured surface and knead until smooth and elastic. Place in a clean bowl, cover, and leave to rise in a warm place until doubled in volume, for about 1½ hours.

4 Grease a baking sheet. Punch down the dough and divide into three equal pieces. Roll to shape each piece into a long thin strip.

5 Begin braiding from the centre strip, tucking in the ends to conceal them. Cover loosely and leave to rise in a warm place for 30 minutes.

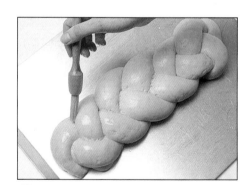

6 Preheat the oven to 190°C/375°F/ Gas 5. Place the bread in a cool place while the oven heats. Brush with the glaze and bake until golden, for 40–45 minutes. Set on a rack to cool completely before serving.

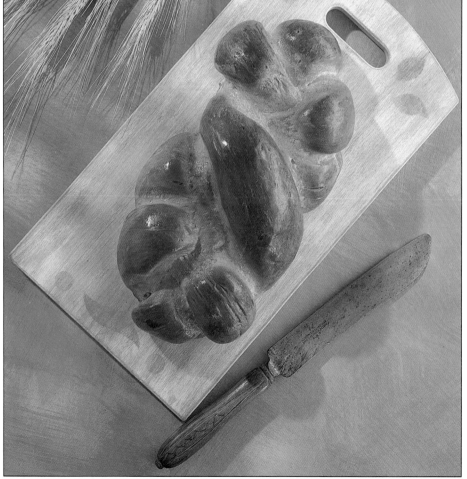

Sesame Seed Bread

Sesame seeds have a distinctive flavour as well as a crunchy texture.

1 Combine the yeast and 150ml/2fl oz/ ¼ cup of the water and leave to dissolve. Mix the flours and salt in a large bowl. Make a well in the centre and pour in the yeast and the remaining water.

2 With a wooden spoon, stir from the centre, incorporating flour with each turn, to obtain a rough dough.

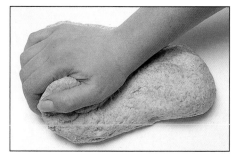

3 Transfer to a floured surface. To knead, push the dough away from you with the palm of your hand, then fold it towards you, and push away again. Repeat until smooth and elastic, then return to the bowl and cover with a plastic bag. Leave in a warm place until doubled in volume, for 1½–2 hours.

4 Grease a 23cm/9in cake tin. Punch down the dough and knead in the sesame seeds. Divide the dough into 16 balls and place in the pan. Cover with a plastic bag and leave in a warm place until risen above the rim of the pan.

5 Preheat the oven to 220°C/425°F/ Gas 7. Brush the top of the loaf with milk and sprinkle with the sesame seeds. Bake for 15 minutes. Lower the heat to 190°C/375°F/Gas 5 and bake until the bottom sounds hollow when tapped, about 30 minutes more. Cool on a rack.

Serves 10–12

10ml/2 tsp active dry yeast
350ml/12fl oz/1½ cups lukewarm water
175g/6oz/1½ cups plain flour
185g/6½oz/1½ cups wholewheat flour
10ml/2 tsp salt
75g/3oz/½ cup toasted sesame seeds
milk, for glazing
30ml/2 tbsp sesame seeds, for sprinkling

NUTRITION NOTES

Per portion

Energy	218Kcals/918kJ
Fat	7.5g
Saturated Fat	1.1g
Cholesterol	0
Fibre	3.6g

Parker House Rolls

These easy-to-make rolls are perfect if you're catering for large numbers.

Makes 48 rolls
10ml/2 tsp active dry yeast
475ml/16fl oz/2 cups lukewarm
skimmed milk
115g/4oz/½ cup margarine
75ml/5 tbsp sugar
10ml/2 tsp salt
2 eggs
790–900g/1¾–2lb/7–8 cups plain flour
60ml/4 tbsp butter

NUTRITION NOTES

Per portion
Energy	114Kcals/479kJ
Fat	3.5g
Saturated Fat	0.68g
Cholesterol	8.5mg
Fibre	0.7g

1 Combine the yeast and 120ml/4fl oz/ ½ cup of milk in a large bowl. Stir and leave for 15 minutes to dissolve. Bring the remaining milk to a simmer, cool for 5 minutes, then beat in the margarine, sugar, salt and eggs. Allow to cool to lukewarm.

2 Pour the milk mixture into the yeast mixture. Stir in 450g/1lb/4 cups of flour with a wooden spoon. Add the remaining flour, 225g/8oz/1 cup at a time, until a rough dough is obtained.

3 Transfer the dough to a lightly floured surface and knead until it is smooth and elastic. Place in a clean bowl, cover with a plastic bag, and leave to rise in a warm place until doubled in volume, for about 2 hours.

4 In a saucepan, melt the butter and set aside. Grease two baking sheets. Punch down the dough and divide into four equal pieces. Roll each piece into a 20 x 30cm/8 x 12in rectangle, about 5mm/¼in thick.

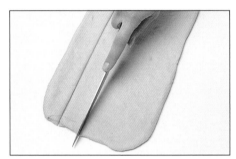

5 Cut each of the rolled-out rectanglular pieces into four 5 x 30cm/2 x 12in strips. Cut each strip into three 10 x 5cm/4 x 2in rectangles.

6 Brush each rectangle with melted butter, then fold the rectangles in half, so that the top extends about 1cm/½in over the bottom.

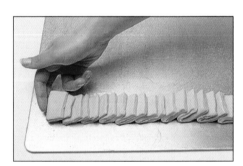

7 Place the rolls slightly overlapping on the baking sheet, with the longer side facing up.

8 Cover and chill for 30 minutes. Preheat the oven to 180°C/350°F/Gas 4. Bake until golden, for 18–20 minutes. Cool the rolls slightly before serving.

Clover Leaf Rolls

Create these clever rolls by baking them in a muffin tin.

1 Heat the milk until lukewarm; test the temperature with your knuckle. Pour into a large bowl and stir in the sugar, butter and yeast. Leave for 15 minutes.

2 Stir the egg and salt into the yeast mixture. Gradually stir in 350g/12oz/ 3⅛ cups of the flour. Add just enough extra flour to obtain a rough dough.

5 Place three balls, side by side, in each muffin cup. Cover loosely and leave to rise in a warm place until doubled in volume, for about half an hour.

6 Preheat the oven to 200°C/400°F/ Gas 6. Brush with glaze. Bake for about 20 minutes, until lightly browned. Cool slightly before serving.

Makes 24
300ml/½ pint/1¼ cups skimmed milk
10ml/2 tbsp sugar
20ml/4 tbsp butter, at room temperature
10ml/2 tsp active dry yeast
1 egg
10ml/2 tsp salt
350–450g/12oz–1lb/3½–4 cups flour
melted butter, for glazing

NUTRITION NOTES
Per portion

Energy	109Kcals/459kJ
Fat	2.9g
Saturated Fat	0.6g
Cholesterol	8mg
Fibre	0.7g

3 Knead on a floured surface until smooth and elastic. Place in a greased bowl, cover, and leave in a warm place until doubled in volume, for about 1½ hours. Grease two 12-cup muffin tins.

4 Punch down the dough. Cut into four equal pieces. Roll each piece into a rope 35cm/14in long. Cut each rope into 18 pieces, then roll each into a ball.

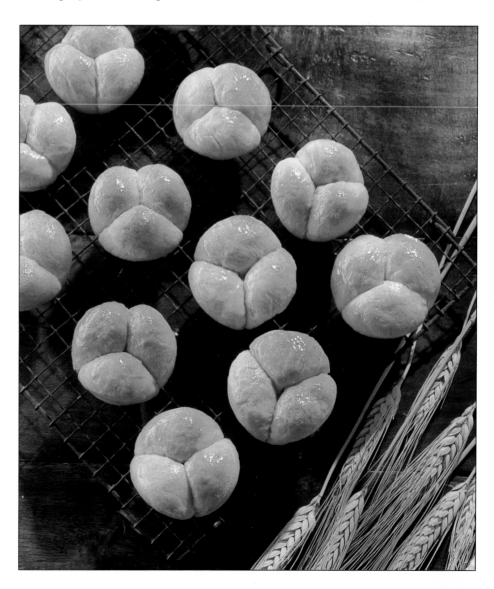

Wholewheat Buttermilk Rolls

These traditional wholewheat rolls are made with buttermilk to keep the fat content low.

Makes 12

10ml/2 tsp active dry yeast
50ml/2fl oz/¼ cup lukewarm water
5ml/1 tsp sugar
175ml/6fl oz/¾ cup lukewarm buttermilk
1.5ml/¼ tsp bicarbonate of soda
5ml/1 tsp salt
45ml/3 tbsp butter, at room temperature
185g/6½oz/1½ cups wholewheat flour
115g/4oz/1 cup plain flour
1 beaten egg, for glazing

NUTRITION NOTES

Per portion

Energy	143Kcals/603kJ
Fat	4.2g
Saturated Fat	0.8g
Cholesterol	17mg
Fibre	2.1g

1 In a large bowl, combine the yeast, water and sugar. Stir, and leave for 15 minutes to dissolve.

2 Add the buttermilk, bicarbonate of soda, salt and butter and stir to blend. Stir in the wholewheat flour.

3 Add just enough of the plain flour to obtain a rough dough. If the dough is stiff, stir it with your hands.

4 Transfer to a floured surface and knead until smooth and elastic. Divide into three equal parts. Roll each into a cylinder, then cut into four.

5 Form the pieces into torpedo shapes. Place on a greased baking sheet, cover, and leave in a warm place until doubled in volume.

6 Preheat the oven to 200°C/400°F/ Gas 6. Brush with the glaze. Bake for 15–20 minutes, until firm. Allow to cool.

French Bread

A French stick is perfect for garlic bread or sandwiches.

1 Combine the yeast and water, stir, and leave for 15 minutes to dissolve. Stir in the salt.

2 Add the flour, 115g/4oz/1 cup at a time. Beat in with a wooden spoon, adding just enough flour to obtain a smooth dough. Alternatively, use an electric mixer with a dough hook attachment.

3 Transfer to a floured surface and knead until smooth and elastic.

4 Shape into a ball, place in a greased bowl, and cover with a plastic bag. Leave to rise in a warm place until doubled in volume, for 2–4 hours.

6 Score the tops in several places with a very sharp knife. Brush with water and place in a cold oven. Set a pan of boiling water on the bottom of the oven and set the oven to 200°C/400°F/Gas 6. Bake until crusty and golden, for about 40 minutes. Cool on a rack.

Serves 16
10ml/2tsp active dry yeast
475ml/16fl oz/2 cups lukewarm water
5ml/1 tsp salt
675–900g/1½–2lb/6–8 cups plain flour
cornmeal, for sprinkling

NUTRITION NOTES
Per portion

Energy	96Kcals/411kJ
Fat	0.37g
Saturated Fat	0.13g
Cholesterol	0
Fibre	0.87g

5 Transfer to a lightly floured board, halve the dough and shape into two long loaves. Place on a baking sheet sprinkled with cornmeal, and let rise for 5 minutes.

Buttermilk Graham Bread

If you can't find graham flour, wholewheat will make an equally delicious loaf.

Serves 8

10ml/2 tsp active dry yeast
120ml/4fl oz/½ cup lukewarm water
225g/8oz/2 cups graham or
wholewheat flour
350g/12oz/3 cups plain flour
130g/4½oz/1 cup cornmeal
10ml/2 tsp salt
30ml/2 tbsp sugar
60ml/4 tbsp butter, at room temperature
475ml/16fl oz/2 cups lukewarm
buttermilk
1 beaten egg, for glazing
sesame seeds, for sprinkling

NUTRITION NOTES

Per portion
Energy	195Kcals/824kJ
Fat	4g
Saturated Fat	0.8g
Cholesterol	10mg
Fibre	1.9g

1 Combine the yeast and water, stir, and leave for 15 minutes to dissolve.

2 Mix together the graham or wholewheat flour, plain flour, cornmeal, salt and sugar in a large bowl. Make a well in the centre of the dry ingredients and pour in the yeast mixture, then add the butter and the buttermilk.

3 Stir from the centre, mixing in the flour until a rough dough is formed. If too stiff, use your hands.

4 Transfer to a floured surface and knead until smooth. Place in a clean bowl, cover, and leave in a warm place until doubled, for 2–3 hours.

5 Grease two 20cm/8in square baking tins. Punch down the dough. Divide into eight equal pieces and roll the pieces into balls. Place four balls in each tin. Cover and leave in a warm place until the dough rises above the rim of the tins, about 1 hour.

6 Preheat the oven to 190°C/375°F/ Gas 5. Brush with the glaze, then sprinkle over the sesame seeds. Bake for about 50 minutes, or until the bottoms sound hollow when tapped. Cool on a wire rack.

Multigrain Bread

Try replacing the wheatgerm or soy flour with rye, barley or buckwheat.

1 Combine the yeast and water, stir, and leave for 15 minutes to dissolve.

2 Place the oats in a large bowl. Heat the milk until scalded, then pour over the oats.

3 Stir in the salt, oil, sugar and honey. Cool the mixture to 29°C/85°F.

4 Stir in the yeast mixture, eggs, wheatgerm, soy and wholewheat flours. Gradually stir in enough plain flour to obtain a rough dough.

5 Transfer the dough to a floured surface and knead, adding flour if necessary, until smooth and elastic. Return to a clean bowl, cover, and leave to rise in a warm place until doubled in volume, for about 2–2½ hours.

6 Grease two 20 x 10cm/8 x 4in bread tins. Punch down the risen dough with your fist and knead briefly.

7 Divide the dough into quarters. Roll each quarter into a cylinder 4cm/1½in thick. Twist together two cylinders and place in a tin; repeat for remaining cylinders.

8 Cover and leave to rise until doubled in size, about 1 hour.

9 Preheat the oven to 190°C/375°F/ Gas 5.

10 Bake the loaves for about 45–50 minutes in the centre of the oven, until the bottoms sound hollow when tapped lightly. Remove from the tins and allow to cool on a rack.

Makes 2 loaves

10ml/2 tsp active dry yeast
50ml/2fl oz/¼ cup lukewarm water
75g/3oz/1 cup rolled oats
475ml/16fl oz/2 cups skimmed milk
10ml/2 tsp salt
50ml/2fl oz/¼ cup oil
50g/2oz/¼ cup brown sugar, firmly packed
30ml/2 tbsp honey
2 eggs, lightly beaten
75g/3oz/½ cup wheatgerm
115g/4oz/1 cup soy flour
225g/8oz/2 cups wholewheat flour
350–400g/12–14oz/3–3½ cups plain flour

NUTRITION NOTES
Per portion

Energy	238Kcals/1007kJ
Fat	4.4g
Saturated Fat	0.64g
Cholesterol	19.7mg
Fibre	4.2g

Austrian Three Grain Bread

A mixture of grains gives this close-textured bread a delightful nutty flavour.
Make two smaller twists, if preferred.

Serves 8–10

475ml/16fl oz/2 cups warm water
10ml/2 tsp dried yeast
pinch of sugar
225g/8oz/2 cups strong white flour
7.5ml/1½ tsp salt
225g/8oz/2 cups malted brown flour
225g/8oz/2 cups rye flour
30ml/2 tbsp linseed
75g/3oz/½ cup medium oatmeal
45ml/3 tbsp sunflower seeds
30ml/2 tbsp malt extract

NUTRITION NOTES

Per portion

Energy	367Kcals/1540kJ
Fat	5.36g
Saturated Fat	0.6g
Cholesterol	0
Fibre	6.67g

1 Put half the water in a jug. Sprinkle the yeast on top. Add the sugar, mix well and leave for 10 minutes.

2 Sift the white flour and salt into a mixing bowl and add the other flours. Set aside 5ml/1 tsp of the linseed and add the rest to the flour mixture with the oatmeal and sunflower seeds. Make a well in the centre. Add the yeast mixture to the bowl with the malt extract and the remaining water.

3 Gradually incorporate the flour.

4 Mix to a soft dough, adding extra water if necessary. Turn out on to a floured surface and knead for about 5 minutes until smooth and elastic. Return to the clean bowl, cover with a damp tea towel and leave to rise for about 2 hours until doubled in bulk.

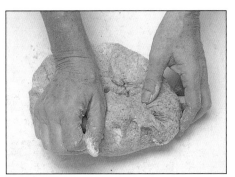

5 Grease a baking sheet. Turn the dough on to a floured surface, knead for 2 minutes, then divide in half. Roll each half into a 30cm/12in long sausage.

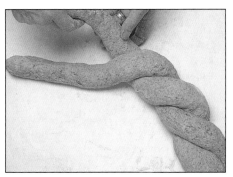

6 Twist the two sausages together, dampen the ends and press to seal. Lift the twist on to the prepared baking sheet. Brush the plait with water, sprinkle with the remaining linseed and cover loosely with a large plastic bag (ballooning it to trap the air inside). Leave in a warm place until well risen. Preheat the oven to 220°C/425°F/Gas 7.

7 Bake the loaf for 10 minutes, then lower the oven temperature to 200°C/400°F/Gas 6 and cook for 20 minutes more, or until the loaf sounds hollow when it is tapped underneath. Transfer to a wire rack to cool.

Granary Baps

These make excellent picnic fare, filled with cottage cheese, tuna, salad and low fat mayonnaise.
They are also very good served warm with soup.

Makes 8

300ml/½ pint/1¼ cups warm water
5ml/1 tsp dried yeast
pinch of sugar
450g/1lb/4 cups malted brown flour
5ml/1 tsp salt
15ml/1 tbsp malt extract
15ml/1 tbsp rolled oats

Cook's Tip
To make a large loaf, shape the dough into a round, flatten it slightly and bake for 30–40 minutes. Test by tapping the base of the loaf – if it sounds hollow, it is cooked.

NUTRITION NOTES

Per portion

Energy	223Kcals/939kJ
Fat	1.14g
Saturated Fat	0.16g
Cholesterol	0
Fibre	3.1g

1 Put half the warm water in a jug. Sprinkle in the yeast. Add the sugar, mix well and leave for 10 minutes.

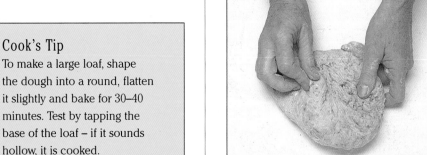

2 Put the malted brown flour and salt in a mixing bowl and make a well in the centre. Add the yeast mixture with the malt extract and the remaining water. Gradually incorporate the flour and mix to a soft dough.

3 Turn the dough on to a floured surface and knead for 5 minutes until smooth and elastic. Return to the clean bowl, cover with a damp tea towel and leave in a warm place to rise for about 2 hours until doubled in bulk.

4 Lightly grease a large baking sheet. Turn the dough on to a floured surface, knead for 2 minutes, then divide into eight pieces. Shape the pieces into balls and flatten them with the palm of your hand to make neat 10cm/4in rounds.

5 Place the rounds on the prepared baking sheets, cover loosely with a large plastic bag (ballooning it to trap the air inside), and leave to stand in a warm place until the baps are well risen. Preheat the oven to 220°C/425°F/Gas 7.

6 Brush the baps with water, sprinkle with the oats and bake for about 20–25 minutes or until they sound hollow when tapped underneath. Cool on a wire rack, then serve with the low fat filling of your choice.

Rye Bread

Rye bread is popular in northern Europe and makes an excellent base for open sandwiches.

Serves 16

350g/12oz/3 cups wholemeal flour
225g/8oz/2 cups rye flour
115g/4oz/1 cup strong white flour
7.5ml/1½ tsp salt
30ml/2 tbsp caraway seeds
475ml/16fl oz/2 cups warm water
10ml/2 tsp dried yeast
pinch of sugar
30ml/2 tbsp molasses

Cook's Tip
To make caraway-seed bread rolls, divide each of the two flattened loaves into eight equal portions. Place them on the baking sheet brush with water and sprinkle with caraway seeds. Vary the topping by using poppy seeds if you prefer.

NUTRITION NOTES
Per portion

Energy	156Kcals/655kJ
Fat	1.2g
Saturated Fat	0.05g
Cholesterol	0
Fibre	4.53g

1 Put the flours and salt in a bowl. Set aside 5ml/1 tsp of the caraway seeds and add the rest to the bowl.

2 Put half the water in a jug. Sprinkle the yeast on top. Add the sugar, mix well and leave for 10 minutes.

3 Make a well in the flour mixture, then add the yeast mixture with the molasses and the remaining water. Gradually incorporate the flour and mix to a soft dough, adding a little extra water if necessary.

4 Transfer to a floured surface and knead for 5 minutes until smooth and elastic. Return to the clean bowl, cover and leave in a warm place for about 2 hours until doubled in bulk. Grease a baking sheet.

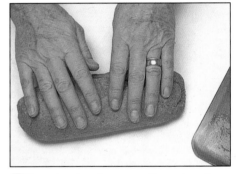

5 Turn the dough on to a floured surface and knead for 2 minutes. Divide the dough in half, then shape into two 23cm/9in long oval loaves. Flatten the loaves slightly and place them on the baking sheet.

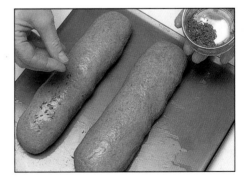

6 Brush the loaves with water and sprinkle with the remaining caraway seeds. Cover and leave in a warm place for about 40 minutes, until well risen. Preheat the oven to 200°C/400°F/Gas 6. Bake the loaves for 30 minutes or until they sound hollow when tapped underneath. Cool on a wire rack. Serve the bread plain, or add a low fat topping.

Cheese Bread

A tasty bread, perfect for making savoury sandwiches.

Serves 10

10ml/2tsp active dry yeast
250ml/8fl oz/1 cup lukewarm skimmed milk
30ml/2 tbsp butter
350g/12oz/3 cups plain flour
10ml/2 tsp salt
115g/4oz/1 cup grated sharp cheddar cheese

NUTRITION NOTES

Per portion

Energy	214Kcals/903kJ
Fat	4.8g
Saturated Fat	1.57g
Cholesterol	5.5mg
Fibre	1.4g

1 Combine the yeast and milk, stir, and leave for 15 minutes to dissolve. Melt the butter, let cool, and add to the yeast mixture.

2 Mix the flour and salt together in a large bowl. Make a well in the centre and pour in the yeast mixture. With a wooden spoon, stir from the centre, incorporating flour with each turn, to obtain a rough dough. If the dough seems too dry, add 30–45ml/ 2–3 tbsp water.

3 Transfer to a floured surface and knead until smooth and elastic. Return to the bowl, cover and leave to rise in a warm place until doubled in volume, for 2–3 hours.

4 Grease a 23 x 13 cm/9 x 5in bread tin. Punch down the dough with your fist. Knead in the cheese, distributing it as evenly as possible.

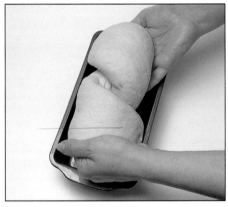

5 Twist the dough, form into a loaf shape and place in the tin, tucking the ends under. Leave to stand in a warm place until the dough rises above the rim of the tin.

6 Preheat the oven to 200°C/400°F/ Gas 6. Bake for 15 minutes, then lower the heat to 190°C/375°F/Gas 5 and bake for about 30 minutes more, until the bottom sounds hollow when tapped. Allow to cool on a rack.

Anadama Bread

A delicious traditional American yeast bread flavoured with molasses.

1 Combine the yeast and lukewarm water, stir well, and leave for 15 minutes to dissolve.

2 Meanwhile, combine the cornmeal, butter or margarine, molasses and boiling water in a large bowl. Add the yeast, egg, and half of the flour. Stir together to blend.

3 Stir in the remaining flour and salt. When the dough becomes too stiff, stir with your hands until it comes away from the sides of the bowl. If it is too sticky, add more flour; if too stiff, add a little water.

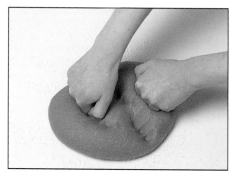

4 Knead until smooth and elastic. Place in a bowl, cover with a plastic bag, and leave in a warm place until doubled in volume, for 2–3 hours.

5 Grease two 69cm x 8cm/27in x 3in bread pans. Punch down the dough with your fist. Shape into two loaves and place in the pans, seam-side down. Cover and leave in a warm place until risen above the top of the pans, for 1–2 hours.

6 Preheat the oven to 375°F. Bake for 50 minutes. Remove and cool on a rack, or set across the pan to cool.

Makes 2 loaves

1 packet active dry yeast
4 tbsp lukewarm water
½ cup cornmeal
3 tbsp butter or margarine
4 tbsp molasses
¾ cup boiling water
1 egg
3 cups flour
2 tsp salt

NUTRITION NOTES
Per portion

Energy	146Kcals/616kJ
Fat	3.1g
Saturated Fat	1.62g
Cholesterol	18.5mg
Fibre	0.9g

Rosemary and Sea Salt Focaccia

Focaccia is an Italian flat bread made with olive oil. Here it is given added flavour with rosemary and coarse sea salt.

Serves 8

350g/12oz/3 cups plain flour
2.5ml/½ tsp salt
10ml/2 tsp easy-blend dried yeast
250ml/8fl oz/1 cup lukewarm water
45ml/3 tbsp olive oil
1 small red onion
leaves from 1 large rosemary sprig
5ml/1 tsp coarse sea salt

1 Sift the flour and salt into a large mixing bowl. Stir in the yeast, then make a well in the middle of the dry ingredients. Pour in the water and 30ml/ 2 tbsp of the oil. Mix well, adding a little more water if the mixture seems too dry.

2 Transfer the dough to a lightly floured surface and knead for about 10 minutes until smooth and elastic.

3 Place the dough in a greased bowl, cover and leave in a warm place for about 1 hour until doubled in size. Knock back and knead the dough for 2–3 minutes.

4 Meanwhile, preheat the oven to 220°C/425°F/Gas 7. Roll out the dough to a large circle about 1cm/½in thick, and transfer to a greased baking sheet. Brush with the remaining oil.

5 Halve the onion and slice it into thin wedges. Sprinkle over the dough with the rosemary and sea salt, pressing lightly.

6 Using a finger, make deep indentations in the dough. Cover the surface with greased clear film. Then leave to rise in a warm place for 30 minutes. Remove the clear film and bake for 25–30 minutes until golden.

NUTRITION NOTES

Per portion
Energy	191Kcals/807kJ
Fat	4.72g
Saturated Fat	0.68g
Cholesterol	0
Fibre	1.46g

Onion Focaccia

This pizza-like flat bread is characterized by its soft dimpled surface.

Makes two 25cm/10in loaves

675/1½lb/6 cups strong plain flour
2.5ml/½ tsp salt
2.5ml/½ tsp caster sugar
15ml/1 tbsp easy-blend dried yeast
60ml/4 tbsp extra virgin olive oil
450ml/¾ pint/1⅞ cups hand-hot water

To finish

2 red onions, thinly sliced
45ml/3 tbsp extra virgin olive oil
15ml/1 tbsp coarse salt

1 Sift the flour, salt and sugar into a large bowl. Stir in the yeast, oil and water and mix to a dough using a round-bladed knife. (Add a little extra water if the dough is dry.)

2 Turn out on to a lightly floured surface and knead for about 10 minutes until smooth and elastic. Put the dough in a clean, lightly oiled bowl and cover with clear film. Leave to rise in a warm place until doubled in bulk.

3 Place two 25cm/10in plain metal flan rings on baking sheets. Oil the sides of the rings and the baking sheets.

4 Preheat the oven to 200°C/400°F/Gas 6. Halve the dough and roll each piece to a 25cm/10in round. Press into the tins, cover with a dampened dish cloth and leave for 30 minutes to rise.

5 Make deep holes, about 2.5cm/1in apart, in the dough. Cover and leave for a further 20 minutes.

6 Scatter with the onions and drizzle over the oil. Sprinkle with the salt, then a little cold water, to stop a crust from forming.

7 Bake for about 25 minutes, sprinkling with water again during cooking. Cool on a wire rack.

NUTRITION NOTES

Per portion

Energy	202Kcals/847kJ
Fat	3.28g
Saturated Fat	0.46g
Cholesterol	0
Fibre	22.13g

Sun-dried Tomato Plait

This is a marvellous Mediterranean-flavoured bread to serve at a summer buffet or barbecue.

Serves 8–10

300ml/½ pint/1¼ cups warm water
5ml/1 tsp dried yeast
pinch of sugar
225g/8oz/2 cups wholemeal flour
225g/8oz/2 cups strong white flour
5ml/1 tsp salt
1.5ml/¼ tsp freshly ground
black pepper
115g/4oz/⅔ cup drained sun-dried
tomatoes in oil, chopped, plus
15ml/1 tbsp oil from the jar
25g/1oz/¼ cup freshly grated
Parmesan cheese
30ml/2 tbsp red pesto
5ml/1 tsp coarse sea salt

Cook's Tip

If you are unable to locate red pesto, use 30ml/2 tbsp chopped fresh basil mixed with 15ml/ 1 tbsp sun-dried tomato paste.

NUTRITION NOTES

Per portion

Energy	294Kcals/1233kJ
Fat	12.12g
Saturated Fat	2.13g
Cholesterol	3.4mg
Fibre	3.39g

1 Put half the warm water in a jug. Sprinkle the yeast on top. Add the sugar, mix well and leave for 10 minutes.

2 Put the wholemeal flour in a mixing bowl. Sift in the white flour, salt and pepper. Make a well in the centre and add the yeast mixture, sun-dried tomatoes, oil, Parmesan, pesto and the remaining water. Gradually incorporate the flour and mix to a soft dough, adding a little extra water if necessary.

3 Transfer the dough to a floured surface and knead for 5 minutes until smooth and elastic. Return to the clean bowl, cover with a damp tea towel and leave in a warm place to rise for about 2 hours until doubled in bulk. Lightly grease a baking sheet.

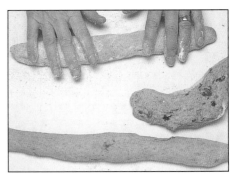

4 Transfer the dough on to a lightly floured surface and knead for a few minutes. Divide the dough into three equal pieces and shape each into a 33cm/12in long sausage.

5 Dampen the ends of the three sausages. Press them together at one end, plait them loosely, then press them together at the other end. Place on the baking sheet, cover and leave in a warm place for 30 minutes until well risen. Preheat the oven to 220°C/ 425°F/Gas 7.

6 Sprinkle the plait with the coarse sea salt. Bake for 10 minutes, then lower the temperature to 200°C/400°F/Gas 6 and bake for a further 15–20 minutes, or until the loaf sounds hollow when tapped underneath. Cool on a wire rack.

Saffron Focaccia

A dazzling yellow bread with a distinctive flavour.

Serves 10

pinch of saffron threads
150ml/¼ pint/⅔ cup boiling water
225g/8oz/2 cups plain flour
2.5ml/½ tsp salt
5ml/1 tsp easy-blend dried yeast
15ml/1 tbsp olive oil

For the topping

2 garlic cloves, sliced
1 red onion, cut into thin wedges
rosemary sprigs
12 black olives, stoned and
coarsely chopped
15ml/1 tbsp olive oil

1 Infuse the saffron in the boiling water. Leave until cooled to lukewarm.

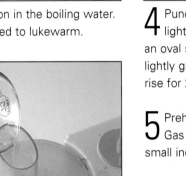

2 Place the flour, salt, yeast and olive oil in a food processor. Turn on and gradually add the saffron and its liquid until the dough forms a ball.

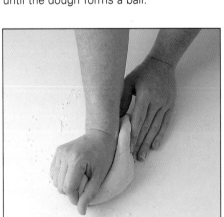

3 Transfer to a floured board and knead for 10–15 minutes. Place in a bowl, cover and leave to rise for about 30–40 minutes, until doubled in size.

4 Punch down the risen dough on a lightly floured surface and roll out into an oval shape, 1cm/½in thick. Place on a lightly greased baking sheet and leave to rise for 20–30 minutes.

5 Preheat the oven to 200°C/400°F/ Gas 6. Use your fingers to press small indentations in the dough.

6 Cover with the topping ingredients, brush lightly with olive oil, and bake for about 25 minutes or until the loaf sounds hollow when tapped on the bottom. Leave to cool.

NUTRITION NOTES

Per portion

Energy	104Kcals/439kJ
Fat	15.91g
Saturated Fat	4g
Cholesterol	0
Fibre	9.4g

Spinach and Bacon Bread

This bread is so tasty that it is a good idea to make double the quantity and freeze one of the loaves.
Use smoked lean back bacon for the best possible flavour with the minimum of fat.

Serves 8

450ml/¾ pint/scant 2 cups warm water
10ml/2 tsp dried yeast
pinch of sugar
15ml/1 tbsp olive oil
1 onion, chopped
115g/4oz rindless smoked bacon rashers, chopped
225g/8oz chopped spinach, thawed if frozen
675g/1½lb/6 cups strong plain flour
7.5ml/1½ tsp salt
7.5ml/1½ tsp grated nutmeg
25g/1oz/¼ cup grated reduced-fat Cheddar cheese

Cook's Tip
If using frozen spinach, be sure to squeeze out any excess liquid or the resulting dough will be too sticky.

NUTRITION NOTES
Per portion
Energy	172Kcals/723kJ
Fat	2.17g
Saturated Fat	0.36g
Cholesterol	1.97mg
Fibre	1.68g

1 Put the water in a bowl. Sprinkle the yeast on top and add the sugar. Mix well and leave for 10 minutes. Lightly grease two 23cm/9in cake tins.

2 Heat the oil in a frying pan and fry the onion and bacon for 10 minutes until golden brown. Meanwhile, if using frozen spinach, drain it thoroughly.

3 Sift the flour, salt and nutmeg into a mixing bowl and make a well in the centre. Add the yeast mixture. Tip in the fried bacon and onion (with the oil), then add the spinach. Gradually incorporate the flour mixture and mix to a soft dough.

4 Transfer the dough to a floured surface and knead for 5 minutes until smooth and elastic. Return to the clean bowl, cover with a damp tea towel and leave in a warm place to rise for about 2 hours, until doubled in bulk.

5 Transfer the dough to a floured surface, knead briefly, then divide it in half. Shape each half into a ball, flatten slightly and place in a tin, pressing the dough so that it extends to the edges. Mark each loaf into eight wedges and sprinkle with the cheese. Cover loosely with a plastic bag and leave in a warm place until well risen. Preheat the oven to 200°C/400°F/Gas 6.

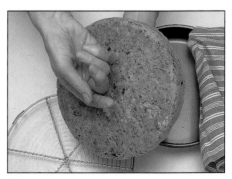

6 Bake the loaves for 25–30 minutes, or until they sound hollow when they are tapped underneath. Transfer to a wire rack to cool.

Parma Ham and Parmesan Bread

This nourishing bread is almost a meal in itself.

Serves 8

225g/8oz/2 cups self-raising wholemeal flour
225g/8oz/2 cups self-raising white flour
5ml/1 tsp baking powder
5ml/1 tsp salt
5ml/1 tsp black pepper
75g/3oz Parma ham
25g/1oz/2 tbsp freshly grated Parmesan cheese
30ml/2 tbsp chopped fresh parsley
45ml/3 tbsp Meaux mustard
350ml/12fl oz/1½ cups buttermilk
skimmed milk, to glaze

NUTRITION NOTES

Per portion
Energy	250Kcals/1053kJ
Fat	3.65g
Saturated Fat	1.3g
Cholesterol	7.09mg
Fibre	3.81g

1 Preheat the oven to 200°C/400°F/ Gas 6. Flour a baking sheet. Place the wholemeal flour in a bowl and sift in the white flour, baking powder and salt. Add the pepper and the ham. Set aside about 15ml/1 tbsp of the grated Parmesan and stir the rest into the flour mixture with the parsley. Make a well in the centre.

2 Mix the mustard and buttermilk, pour into the flour and quickly mix to a soft dough.

3 Transfer the dough to a floured surface and knead briefly. Shape into an oval loaf, brush with milk and sprinkle with the reserved Parmesan cheese. Put the loaf on the prepared baking sheet.

4 Bake the loaf for 25–30 minutes, or until it sounds hollow when tapped underneath. Allow to cool before serving.

Caraway Breadsticks

Ideal to nibble with drinks, these can be made with all sorts of other seeds –
try cumin seeds, poppy seeds or celery seeds.

1 Grease two baking sheets. Put the warm water in a jug. Sprinkle the yeast on top. Add the sugar, mix well and leave for 10 minutes.

2 Sift the flour and salt into a mixing bowl, stir in the caraway seeds and make a well in the centre. Add the yeast mixture and gradually incorporate the flour to make a soft dough, adding a little water if necessary.

3 Preheat the oven to 220°C/425°F/ Gas 7. Transfer the dough to a lightly floured surface and knead for 5 minutes until smooth. Divide the mixture into 20 pieces and roll each piece into a 30cm/12in stick.

4 Arrange the sticks on the baking sheets, leaving room between them to allow for rising.

5 Bake the breadsticks for about 10–12 minutes until golden brown. Cool on the baking sheets.

Makes about 20

150ml/¼ pint/⅔ cup warm water
2.5ml/½ tsp dried yeast
pinch of sugar
225g/8oz/2 cups plain flour
2.5ml/½ tsp salt
10ml/2 tsp caraway seeds

NUTRITION NOTES

Per portion

Energy	45Kcals/189kJ
Fat	0.24g
Saturated Fat	0.02g
Cholesterol	0
Fibre	0.3g

Cheese and Onion Sticks

An extremely tasty bread which is very good with soups or salads. Use an extra-strong cheese to give plenty of flavour without piling on the fat.

Serves 8–12

300ml/½ pint/1¼ cups warm water
5ml/1 tsp dried yeast
pinch of sugar
15ml/1 tbsp sunflower oil
1 red onion, finely chopped
450g/1lb/4 cups strong white flour
5ml/1 tsp salt
5ml/1 tsp dry mustard
45ml/3 tbsp chopped fresh herbs, such as thyme, parsley, marjoram or sage
75g/3oz/¾ cup grated reduced-fat Cheddar cheese

Cook's Tip
To make Onion and Coriander Sticks, omit the cheese, herbs and mustard. Add 15ml/1 tbsp ground coriander and 45ml/3 tbsp chopped fresh coriander instead.

NUTRITION NOTES
Per portion

Energy	210Kcals/882kJ
Fat	3.16g
Saturated Fat	0.25g
Cholesterol	3.22mg
Fibre	1.79g

1 Put the water in a jug. Sprinkle the yeast on top. Add the sugar, mix well and leave for 10 minutes.

2 Heat the oil in a small frying pan and fry the onion until it is well coloured.

3 Stir the flour, salt and mustard into a mixing bowl, then add the chopped herbs. Set aside 30ml/2 tbsp of the cheese. Stir the rest into the flour mixture and make a well in the centre. Add the yeast mixture with the fried onions and oil, then gradually incorporate the flour and mix to a soft dough, adding extra water if necessary.

4 Transfer the dough to a floured surface and knead for 5 minutes until smooth and elastic. Return to the clean bowl, cover with a damp tea towel and leave in a warm place to rise for about 2 hours, until doubled in bulk. Lightly grease two baking sheets.

5 Transfer the dough on to a floured surface, knead briefly, then divide the mixture in half and roll each piece into a 30cm/12in long stick. Place each stick on a baking sheet and make diagonal cuts along the top.

6 Sprinkle the sticks with the reserved cheese. Cover and leave for 30 minutes until well risen. Preheat the oven to 220°C/425°F/Gas 7. Bake the sticks for 25 minutes or until they sound hollow when tapped underneath.

Saffron and Basil Breadsticks

Saffron lends its delicate aroma and flavour, as well as rich yellow colour, to these tasty breadsticks.

Makes 32

generous pinch of saffron strands
30ml/2 tbsp hot water
450g/1lb/4 cups strong white flour
5ml/1 tsp salt
10ml/2 tsp easy-blend dried yeast
300ml/½ pint/1¼ cups lukewarm water
45ml/3 tbsp olive oil
45ml/3 tbsp chopped fresh basil

1 Infuse the saffron strands in the hot water for 10 minutes.

2 Sift the flour and salt into a large mixing bowl. Stir in the yeast, then make a well in the centre of the dry ingredients. Pour in the lukewarm water and saffron liquid and start to mix a little.

3 Add the oil and basil and continue to mix to a soft dough.

4 Turn out and knead the dough on a lightly floured surface for about 10 minutes until smooth and elastic. Place in a greased bowl, cover with clear film and leave for about 1 hour until it has doubled in size.

5 Knock back and knead the dough on a lightly floured surface for 2–3 minutes.

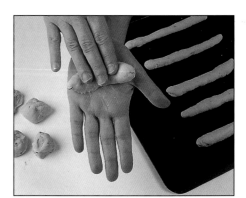

6 Preheat the oven to 220°C/425°F/ Gas 7. Divide the dough into 32 pieces and shape into long sticks. Place well apart on greased baking sheets, then leave for a further 15–20 minutes until they become puffy. Bake for about 15 minutes until crisp and golden. Serve warm.

NUTRITION NOTES

Per portion

Energy	59Kcals/249kJ
Fat	1.3g
Saturated Fat	1.17g
Cholesterol	0
Fibre	0.4g

Cook's Tip

Use powdered saffron if saffron strands are not available. Turmeric is an inexpensive alternative: it imparts a lovely gold colour, but its flavour is not as delicate.

Olive and Herb Bread

Olive breads are popular all over the Mediterranean. For this Greek recipe use rich oily olives
or those marinated in herbs rather than canned ones.

Serves 20

2 red onions, thinly sliced
30ml/2 tbsp olive oil
225g/8oz/1½ cups pitted black or
green olives
750g/1¾lb/7 cups strong plain flour
7.5ml/1½ tsp salt
20ml/4 tsp easy-blend dried yeast
45ml/3 tbsp roughly chopped parsley,
coriander or mint
457ml/16fl oz/2 cups hand-hot water

NUTRITION NOTES

Per portion
Energy	157Kcals/664kJ
Fat	2.9g
Saturated Fat	0.41g
Cholesterol	0
Fibre	1.8g

---

1 Fry the onions in the oil until soft.
Roughly chop the olives.

2 Put the flour, salt, yeast and parsley,
coriander or mint in a large bowl with
the olives and fried onions and pour in
the water. Mix to a dough using a round-
bladed knife, adding a little more water if
the mixture feels dry.

3 Transfer to a lightly floured surface
and knead for about 10 minutes.
Put in a clean bowl, cover with clear
film and leave in a warm place until
doubled in bulk.

4 Preheat the oven to 220°C/425°F/
Gas 7. Lightly grease two baking
sheets. Turn the dough on to a floured
surface and cut in half. Shape into two
rounds and place on the baking sheets.
Cover loosely with lightly oiled clear film
and leave until doubled in size.

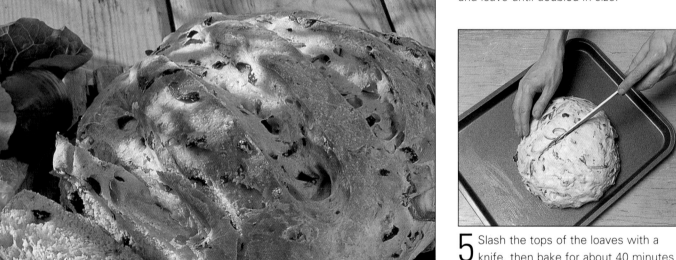

5 Slash the tops of the loaves with a
knife, then bake for about 40 minutes
or until the loaves sound hollow when
tapped on the bottom. Transfer to a wire
rack to cool.

Variation

Shape the dough into 16 small rolls.
Slash the tops as above and reduce
the cooking time to 25 minutes.

Tomato Breadsticks

Once you've tried this simple recipe, you'll never buy manufactured breadsticks again.
Serve as a snack, or with aperitifs and a dip at the beginning of a meal.

1 Place the flour, salt and yeast in a food processor. Add the honey and olive oil and, with the machine running, gradually pour in the water (you may not need it all as flours vary). Stop adding water as soon as the dough starts to cling together. Process for 1 minute more.

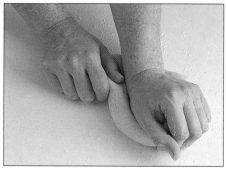

2 Transfer the dough to a floured board and knead for 3–4 minutes until springy and smooth.

3 Knead in the chopped sun-dried tomatoes. Form into a ball and place in a lightly oiled bowl. Leave to rise for 5 minutes.

4 Preheat the oven to 150°C/300°F/ Gas 2. Divide the dough into sixteen pieces and roll each piece into a 28 x 1cm/ 11 x ½in long stick. Place on a lightly oiled baking sheet and leave to rise in a warm place for 15 minutes.

5 Brush the sticks with milk and sprinkle with poppy seeds. Bake for 30 minutes. Leave to cool on a wire cooling rack.

Makes 16

225g/8oz/2 cups plain flour
2.5ml/½ tsp salt
2.5ml/½ tsp easy-blend dried yeast
5ml/1 tsp honey
5ml/1 tsp olive oil
150ml/¼ pint/⅔ cup warm water
6 halves sun-dried tomatoes in olive oil, drained and chopped
15ml/1 tbsp skimmed milk
10ml/2 tsp poppy seeds

NUTRITION NOTES
Per portion

Energy	82Kcals/346kJ
Fat	3.53g
Saturated Fat	0.44g
Cholesterol	0
Fibre	0.44g

Cook's Tip
Instead of sun-dried tomatoes, you could try making these breadsticks with reduced fat Cheddar cheese, sesame seeds or herbs.

Sourdough Bread

Sourdough bread has a slightly sour, tangy flavour created by using a special yeast starter as the leavener.

Serves 10
350g/12oz/3 cups flour
15ml/1 tbsp salt
120ml/4fl oz/½ cup lukewarm water

For the starter
5ml/1 tsp active dry yeast
175ml/6fl oz/¾ cup lukewarm water
50g/2oz/½ cup flour

Cook's Tip
The starter can be chilled for up to one week, but must be brought back to room temperature before using.

NUTRITION NOTES
Per portion
Energy	179Kcals/763kJ
Fat	0.7g
Saturated Fat	0.1g
Cholesterol	0
Fibre	1.6g

1 For the starter, combine the yeast and water, stir and leave for 15 minutes to dissolve.

2 Sprinkle over the flour and whisk until it forms a batter; it does not have to be smooth. Cover and leave to rise in a warm place for at least 24 hours, or preferably 2–4 days, before using.

3 For the bread, combine the flour and salt in a large bowl. Make a well in the centre and add the starter and water. With a wooden spoon, stir from the centre, incorporating more flour with each turn, to obtain a rough dough.

4 Transfer the dough to a floured surface. To knead, push the dough away from you with the palm of your hand, then fold it towards you, and push it away again. Repeat the process until the dough has become smooth and elastic.

5 Place in a clean bowl, cover, and leave to rise in a warm place until doubled in volume, for about 2 hours. Lightly grease a 20 x 10cm/8 x 4in bread tin.

6 Punch down the dough with your fist. Knead briefly, then form into a loaf shape and place in the tin, seam-side down. Cover with a plastic bag, and leave to rise in a warm place until the dough rises above the rim of the tin, for about 1½ hours.

7 Preheat the oven to 220°C/425°F/ Gas 7. Dust the top of the loaf with flour, then score lengthways. Bake for 15 minutes. Lower the heat to 190°C/ 375°F/Gas 5 and bake for about 30 minutes more, or until the bottom sounds hollow when tapped.

Potato Bread

A recipe for a traditional loaf – that is low in fat.

Serves 16
60ml/4 tsp active dry yeast
250ml/8fl oz/1 cup lukewarm
skimmed milk
675g/½lb potatoes, boiled (reserve
250ml/8fl oz/1 cup of potato
cooking liquid)
30ml/2 tbsp oil
20ml/4 tsp salt
675–790g/1½–1¾lb/6–6½ cups flour

NUTRITION NOTES
Per portion
Energy	177Kcals/751kJ
Fat	1.7g
Saturated Fat	0.2g
Cholesterol	0
Fibre	1.5g

1 Combine the yeast and the milk in a large bowl and leave to dissolve for about 15 minutes. Mash the potatoes.

2 Add the potatoes, oil and salt to the yeast mixture and mix well. Stir in 250ml/8fl oz/1 cup of the cooking water, then stir in the flour, 115g/4oz/1 cup at a time, to form a stiff dough.

3 Transfer to a floured surface and knead until smooth and elastic. Return to the bowl, cover and leave in a warm place until doubled in size, for 1–1½ hours. Punch down, then leave to rise for another 40 minutes.

4 Grease two 23 x 13cm/9 x 5in loaf tins. Roll the dough into 20 small balls. Place two rows of balls in each tin. Leave until the dough has risen above the rim of the tins.

5 Preheat the oven to 200°C/400°F/ Gas 6. Bake for 10 minutes, then lower the heat to 190°C/375°F/Gas 5 and bake for about 40 minutes, or until the bottoms sound hollow when tapped. Cool on a rack.

Irish Soda Bread

This is a solid bread – delicious with salad and pickles.

1 Preheat the oven to 200°C/400°F/ Gas 6. Grease a baking sheet.

2 Sift the flours, bicarbonate of soda and salt together in a bowl. Make a well in the centre and add the butter or margarine and buttermilk. Working outward from the centre, stir with a fork until a soft dough is formed.

6 Dust with flour. Bake until brown, for 40–50 minutes. Transfer to a rack to cool.

Serves 10

225g/8oz/2 cups plain flour
225g/8oz/1 cup wholewheat flour
5ml/1 tsp bicarbonate of soda
5ml/1 tsp salt
30ml/2 tbsp butter or margarine, at room temperature
350ml/12fl oz/1½ cups buttermilk
15ml/1 tbsp plain flour, for dusting

NUTRITION NOTES

Per portion

Energy	188Kcals/797kJ
Fat	3.3g
Saturated Fat	0.7g
Cholesterol	1mg
Fibre	2.3g

3 With floured hands, gather the dough into a ball.

4 Transfer to a floured surface and knead for 3 minutes. Shape the dough into a large round.

5 Place on the baking sheet. Cut a cross in the top with a sharp knife.

Brown Soda Bread

This is very easy to make - simply mix and bake. Instead of yeast, bicarbonate of soda and cream of tartar are the raising agents. This is an excellent recipe for those new to bread making.

Serves 20
450/1lb/4 cups plain flour
450/1lb/4 cups wholemeal flour
10ml/2 tsp salt
15ml/1 tbsp bicarbonate of soda
20ml/4 tsp cream of tartar
10ml/2 tsp caster sugar
50g/2oz/4 tbsp butter
up to 900ml/1½ pints/3¾ cups
buttermilk or skimmed milk
extra wholemeal flour, to sprinkle

NUTRITION NOTES
Per portion
Energy	185Kcals/784kJ
Fat	2.9g
Saturated Fat	0.53g
Cholesterol	1.1mg
Fibre	2.8g

1 Lightly grease a baking sheet. Preheat the oven to 190°C/375°F/Gas 5.

2 Sift all the dry ingredients into a large bowl, tipping any bran from the flour back into the bowl.

3 Rub the butter into the flour mixture, then add enough buttermilk or milk to make a soft dough. You may not need all of it, so add it cautiously.

4 Knead the dough lightly until smooth – do not overknead – then transfer to the baking sheet and shape to a large round about 5cm/2in thick.

5 Using the floured handle of a wooden spoon, make a large cross on top of the dough. Sprinkle over a little extra wholemeal flour.

6 Bake for 40–50 minutes until risen and firm. Cool for 5 minutes before transferring to a wire rack to cool further.

Sage Soda Bread

This wonderful loaf, quite unlike bread made with yeast, has a velvety texture and a powerful sage aroma.

1 Preheat the oven to 220°C/425°F/ Gas 7. Sift the dry ingredients into a mixing bowl.

2 Stir in the sage and add enough buttermilk to make a soft dough.

3 Shape the dough into a round loaf with your hands and place on a lightly oiled baking sheet.

4 Cut a deep cross in the top. Bake in the oven for about 40 minutes until the loaf is well risen and sounds hollow when tapped on the bottom. Leave to cool on a wire rack.

Serves 10

175g/6oz/1½ cups wholemeal flour
115g/4oz/1 cup strong white flour
2.5ml/½ tsp salt
5ml/1 tsp bicarbonate of soda
30ml/2 tbsp shredded fresh sage or
10ml/2 tsp dried sage
300–450ml/½–¾ pint/1¼ scant
cups buttermilk

NUTRITION NOTES
Per portion
Energy	125Kcals/525kJ
Fat	9.2g
Saturated Fat	0.2g
Cholesterol	0.7mg
Fibre	2.81g

Cook's Tip
As an alternative to the sage, try using either finely chopped rosemary or thyme.

Spiral Herb Bread

An attractive and delicious bread that is ideal for serving with a salad for a healthy lunch.

Serves 20

30ml/2 tbsp easy-blend dried yeast
600ml/1 pint/2½ cups lukewarm water
425g/15oz/3⅔ cups strong white flour
15ml/1 tbsp salt
25g/1oz/2 tbsp sunflower margarine
large bunch of parsley, finely chopped
bunch of spring onions, chopped
garlic clove, finely chopped
salt and freshly ground black pepper
1 egg, lightly beaten
skimmed milk, for glazing

NUTRITION NOTES

Per portion
Energy	85Kcals/356kJ
Fat	1.22g
Saturated Fat	0.49g
Cholesterol	7.24mg
Fibre	1.54g

1 Combine the yeast with approximately 50ml/2fl oz/¼ cup of the water, stir and leave to dissolve. Mix together the flour and salt in a large bowl. Make a well in the centre and pour in the yeast mixture and the remaining water. With a wooden spoon, stir from the centre, working outwards to obtain a rough dough.

2 Transfer the dough to a floured surface and knead until smooth and elastic. Return to the bowl, cover with a plastic bag, and leave for about 2 hours until doubled in volume.

3 Meanwhile, combine the margarine, parsley, spring onions and garlic in a large frying pan. Cook over a low heat, stirring until softened. Season with salt and pepper and set aside.

4 Grease two 23 x 13cm/9 x 5in loaf tins. When the dough has risen, cut in half and roll each half into a rectangle about 35 x 23cm/14 x 9in. Brush both with the beaten egg. Divide the herb mixture between the two, spreading just up to the edges.

5 Roll up to enclose the filling and pinch the short ends to seal. Place in the tins, seam-side down. Cover the dough with a clean tea towel and leave undisturbed in a warm place until the dough rises above the rim of the tins.

6 Preheat the oven to 190°C/375°F/ Gas 5. Brush the loaves with milk and bake for about 55 minutes, until the bottoms sound hollow when tapped. Cool on a wire rack.

Walnut Bread

Delicious at any time of day, this bread may be eaten plain or topped with low fat cream cheese.

1 Mix together the flours and salt in a large bowl. Make a well in the centre and pour in 250ml/8fl oz/1 cup of the water, the honey and the yeast. Set aside until the yeast dissolves and the mixture is frothy.

2 Add the remaining water. With a wooden spoon, stir from the centre, incorporating flour with each turn, to obtain a smooth dough. Add more flour to the bowl if the dough is too sticky and use your hands if the dough becomes too stiff to stir.

3 Transfer to a floured board and knead, adding flour if necessary, until the dough is smooth and elastic. Place in a greased bowl and roll the dough around in the bowl to coat thoroughly all over.

6 Preheat the oven to 220°C/425°F/Gas 7. With a sharp knife, score the top of the loaf and brush with the egg glaze. Bake for 15 minutes. Lower the temperature to 190°C/375°F/Gas 5 and bake for about 40 minutes, or until the bottom of the loaf sounds hollow when tapped. Leave to cool.

Serves 10

425g/15oz/3⅔ cups wholemeal flour
150g/5oz/1¼ cups strong white flour
12.5ml/2½ tsp salt
525ml/18fl oz/2¼ cups lukewarm water
15ml/1 tbsp clear honey
15ml/1 tbsp easy-blend dried yeast
150g/5oz/1¼ cups walnut pieces, plus more for decorating
1 egg, beaten, for glazing

NUTRITION NOTES
Per portion

Energy	285Kcals/1198kJ
Fat	10.93g
Saturated Fat	1.2g
Cholesterol	7.7mg
Fibre	4.7g

4 Cover with a plastic bag and leave in a warm place until doubled in volume, about 1½ hours.

5 Punch down the dough very firmly and knead in the walnuts. Shape the dough into a round loaf and place on a greased baking sheet. Press in the walnut pieces to decorate the top. Cover loosely with a damp tea towel and leave in a warm place for about 25–30 minutes until doubled in size.

Oatmeal Bread

A healthy bread with a delightfully crumbly texture due to the inclusion of rolled oats.

Serves 20

475ml/16fl oz/2 cups skimmed milk
25g/1oz/2 tbsp low fat margarine
50g/2oz/1¼ cups dark brown sugar
10ml/2 tsp salt
15ml/1 tbsp easy-blend dried yeast
50ml/2fl oz/¼ cup lukewarm water
400g/14oz/3½ cups rolled oats
450–675g/1–1½lb/4–6 cups strong white flour

NUTRITION NOTES

Per portion

Energy	228Kcals/958kJ
Fat	3.44g
Saturated Fat	1.19g
Cholesterol	3.9mg
Fibre	2.41g

1 Scald the milk. Remove from the heat and stir in the margarine, sugar and salt. Leave until lukewarm.

2 Combine the yeast and lukewarm water in a large bowl and leave until the yeast is dissolved and the mixture is frothy. Stir in the milk mixture.

3 Add 275g/10oz/2½ cups of the oats and enough flour to obtain a soft pliable dough.

4 Transfer to a floured surface and knead until smooth and elastic.

5 Place the dough in a greased bowl, cover with a plastic bag, and leave for about 2–3 hours, until doubled in volume. Grease a large baking sheet.

6 Transfer the dough to a lightly floured surface and divide in half.

7 Shape into rounds. Place on the baking sheet, cover with a damp tea towel and leave to rise for about 1 hour, until doubled in volume.

8 Preheat the oven to 200°C/400°F/ Gas 6. Score the tops of the loaves and sprinkle with the remaining oats. Bake for about 45–50 minutes, until the bottoms sound hollow when tapped. Cool on wire racks.

Courgette and Walnut Loaf

A moist and crunchy loaf – a real treat.

1 Preheat the oven to 180°C/350°F/ Gas 4. Grease the base and sides of a 900g/2lb loaf tin and line with grease-proof paper.

2 Beat the eggs and sugar together and gradually add the oil.

3 Sift the flour into a bowl together with the baking powder, bicarbonate of soda, cinnamon and allspice.

4 Mix into the egg mixture with the rest of the ingredients, reserving 15ml/1 tbsp of the sunflower seeds for the top.

5 Spoon into the loaf tin, level off the top, and sprinkle with the reserved sunflower seeds.

6 Bake for about 1 hour or until a skewer inserted in the centre comes out clean. Leave to cool slightly, then turn out on to a wire cooling rack.

Serves 10

3 eggs
75g/3oz/½ cup light brown sugar
50ml/2fl oz/¼ cup sunflower oil
225g/8oz/1½ cups wholemeal flour
5ml/1 tsp baking powder
5ml/1 tsp bicarbonate of soda
5ml/1 tsp ground cinnamon
2.5ml/½ tsp ground allspice
7.5ml/½ tbsp green cardamoms, seeds removed and crushed
150g/5oz/1 cup coarsely grated courgette
50g/2oz/¼ cup walnuts, chopped
50g/2oz/¼ cup sunflower seeds

NUTRITION NOTES

Per portion
Energy	307Kcals/1290kJ
Fat	20.19g
Saturated Fat	2.64g
Cholesterol	65.45mg
Fibre	2.86g

Italian Flat Bread with Sage

This bread is perfect served hot to accompany a pasta supper.

Serves 10

10ml/2 tsp active dry yeast
250ml/8fl oz/1 cup lukewarm water
375g/12oz/3 cups plain flour
10ml/2 tsp salt
75ml/5 tbsp extra virgin olive oil
12 fresh sage leaves, chopped

NUTRITION NOTES
Per portion
Energy	205Kcals/864kJ
Fat	6.1g
Saturated Fat	0.6g
Cholesterol	0
Fibre	1.4g

1 Combine the yeast and water, stir and leave for 15 minutes to dissolve.

2 Mix the flour and salt in a large bowl, and make a well in the centre.

3 Stir in the yeast mixture and 60ml/ 4 tbsp of the oil. Stir from the centre, incorporating flour with each turn, to obtain a rough dough.

4 Transfer to a floured surface and knead until smooth and elastic. Place in a lightly oiled bowl. Cover and leave to rise in a warm place until doubled in volume, for about 2 hours.

5 Preheat the oven to 200°C/400°F/ Gas 6 and place a baking sheet in the centre of the oven.

6 Punch down the dough. Knead in the sage leaves, then roll into a 30cm/12in round. Leave to rise slightly.

7 Dimple the surface all over with your finger. Drizzle the remaining oil on top. Slide a floured board under the bread, carry to the oven, and slide off on to the hot baking sheet. Bake for about 35 minutes, or until golden brown. Cool on a rack.

Courgette Yeast Bread

The grated courgettes give extra moisture to this tasty loaf.

Serves 10

450g/1lb/3½ cups courgettes, grated
30ml/2 tbsp salt
10ml/2tsp active dry yeast
300ml/½ pint/1¼ cups lukewarm water
400g/14oz/3½ cups plain flour
olive oil, for brushing

NUTRITION NOTES

Per portion

Energy	191Kcals/811kJ
Fat	1.2g
Saturated Fat	0.2g
Cholesterol	0
Fibre	2g

1 In a colander, alternate layers of grated courgettes and salt. Leave for 30 minutes, then squeeze out the moisture with your hands.

2 Combine the yeast with 50ml/2fl oz/ ¼ cup of the lukewarm water, stir and leave for 15 minutes to dissolve the yeast.

3 Place the courgettes, yeast and flour in a bowl. Stir together and add just enough of the remaining water to obtain a rough dough.

4 Transfer to a floured surface and knead until smooth and elastic. Return the dough to the bowl, cover with a plastic bag, and leave to rise in a warm place until doubled in volume, for about 1½ hours.

5 Grease a baking sheet. Punch down the risen dough with your fist and knead into a tapered cylinder. Place on the baking sheet, cover and leave to rise in a warm place until doubled in volume, for about 45 minutes.

6 Preheat the oven to 220°C/425°F/ Gas 7. Brush the bread with olive oil and bake for about 40–45 minutes, or until the loaf is a golden colour. Cool on a rack before serving.

Rosemary Bread

Sliced thinly, this herb bread is delicious with soup for a light meal.

Serves 10

7g/¼ oz dried fast-action yeast
175g/6oz/1½ cups wholemeal flour
175g/6oz/1½ cups self-raising flour
10ml/2 tsp butter, melted, plus extra to
grease bowl and tin
50ml/2fl oz/¼ cup warm water
250ml/8fl oz/1 cup skimmed milk, at
room temperature
15ml/1 tbsp sugar
5ml/1 tsp salt
15ml/1 tbsp sesame seeds
15ml/1 tbsp dried chopped onion
15ml/1 tbsp fresh rosemary leaves,
plus extra to decorate
115g/4oz/1 cup cubed Cheddar cheese
coarse salt, to decorate

NUTRITION NOTES

Per portion

Energy	188Kcals/795kJ
Fat	5.6g
Saturated Fat	1.7g
Cholesterol	6mg
Fibre	2.2g

1 Mix the fast-action yeast with the flours in a large mixing bowl. Add the melted butter. Stir in the warm water, milk, sugar, salt, sesame seeds, onion and rosemary. Knead thoroughly until quite smooth.

2 Flatten the dough, then add the cheese cubes. Quickly knead them in until they are well combined.

3 Place the dough into a large clean bowl greased with a little butter, turning it so that it becomes lightly greased on all sides. Cover with a clean, dry cloth. Put the greased bowl and dough in a warm place for about 1½ hours, or until the dough has risen and doubled in size.

4 Grease a 23 x 13cm/9 x 5in loaf tin with the remaining butter. Knock down the dough to remove some of the air, and shape it into a loaf. Put the loaf into the tin, cover with the clean cloth used earlier and leave for about 1 hour until it has doubled in size once again. Preheat the oven to 190°C/375°F/Gas 5.

5 Bake for 30 minutes. During the last 5–10 minutes of baking, cover the loaf with silver foil to prevent it from becoming too dark. Remove from the loaf tin and leave to cool on a wire rack. Decorate with rosemary leaves and coarse salt scattered on top.

Dill Bread

Herb bread makes a tasty change at any mealtime.

1 Mix together the yeast, water and sugar in a large bowl and leave for 15 minutes to dissolve.

2 Stir in 350g/12lb/3 cups of the flour. Cover and leave to rise in a warm place for 45 minutes.

3 Cook the onion in 15ml/1 tbsp of the oil until soft. Set aside to cool, then stir into the yeast mixture. Stir in the dill, eggs, cottage cheese, salt and remaining oil into the yeast mixture. Gradually add the remaining flour until too stiff to stir.

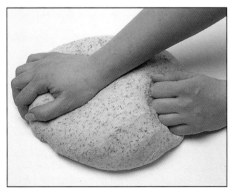

4 Transfer to a floured surface and knead until smooth and elastic. Place in a bowl, cover, and leave to rise until doubled in volume, for 1–1½ hours.

5 Grease a large baking sheet. Cut the dough in half and shape into two rounds. Leave to rise in a warm place for 30 minutes.

6 Preheat the oven to 190°C/375°F/ Gas 5. Score the tops, brush with the milk, and bake until browned, about 50 minutes. Cool on a rack.

Serves 20

20ml/4 tsp active dry yeast
475ml/16fl oz/2 cups lukewarm water
30ml/2 tbsp sugar
850g/1lb 14oz/7½ cups plain flour
½ onion, chopped
60ml/4 tbsp oil
1 large bunch of dill, finely chopped
2 eggs, lightly beaten
115g/4oz/½ cup cottage cheese
20ml/4 tsp salt
milk, for glazing

NUTRITION NOTES

Per portion

Energy	237Kcals/1003kJ
Fat	3.7g
Saturated Fat	0.6g
Cholesterol	20mg
Fibre	1.8g

Naan

There are various recipes for making naan, but this one is particularly easy to follow. Always serve naan warm, preferably straight from the grill, or wrap them in foil until you are ready to serve the meal.

Makes 6

5ml/1 tsp caster sugar
5ml/1 tsp dried yeast
150ml/¼ pint/⅔ cup warm water
225g/8oz/2 cups plain flour
5ml/1 tsp ghee or butter
5ml/1 tsp salt
50g/2oz/¼ cup low fat margarine, melted
5ml/1 tsp poppy seeds

NUTRITION NOTES

Per portion
Energy	177Kcals/744kJ
Fat	5.07g
Saturated Fat	1.24g
Cholesterol	0.5mg
Fibre	0.2g

1 Put the sugar and yeast in a small bowl, add the warm water and mix well until the yeast has dissolved. Leave for 10 minutes or until the mixture becomes frothy.

2 Place the flour in a large mixing bowl, make a well in the middle and add the ghee or butter, and salt, then pour in the yeast mixture.

3 Mix well, using your hands, to make a dough, adding some more water if the dough is too dry. Turn out on to a floured surface and knead for about 5 minutes or until smooth.

4 Place the dough back in the clean bowl, cover with foil and leave to rise in a warm place for 1½ hours or until doubled in size.

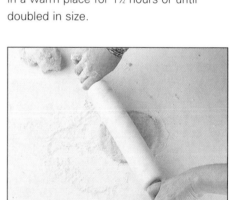

5 Preheat the grill to very hot. Transfer the dough to a floured surface and knead for a further two minutes. Break off small balls with your hand and roll into rounds about 12cm/5in in diameter and 1cm/½in thick.

6 Place on a sheet of greased foil and grill for 7–10 minutes, turning twice to brush with margarine and sprinkle with poppy seeds.

Wholemeal Chapatis

These Indian breads are best served hot from the pan – but can be kept warm in foil.

1 Place the flour and salt in a mixing bowl. Make a well in the middle and gradually stir in the water, mixing well with your fingers.

2 Form a supple dough and knead for 7–10 minutes. Ideally, cover with clear film and leave on one side for 15–20 minutes. If time is short, roll out straight away.

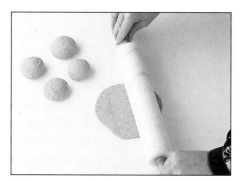

3 Divide the dough into 8–10 equal portions. Roll out each piece to a round on a well-floured surface.

4 Place a heavy-based frying pan over a high heat. When steam rises from it, lower the heat to medium and add the first chapati to the pan.

5 When the chapati begins to bubble, turn it over. Press down with a clean tea towel or a flat spoon and turn once again. Remove from the pan and keep warm in foil. Repeat the process until all the chapatis are cooked.

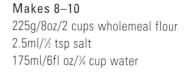

Makes 8–10
225g/8oz/2 cups wholemeal flour
2.5ml/½ tsp salt
175ml/6fl oz/¾ cup water

NUTRITION NOTES
Per portion
Energy	87Kcals/366kJ
Fat	0.62g
Saturated Fat	0.08g
Cholesterol	0
Fibre	1.3g

Teabreads

These light and tasty
teabreads use the natural
sweetness of fruit and
honey for a mid-afternoon
energy-boosting treat that
won't weigh you down.

Banana and Cardamom Bread

The combination of banana and cardamom is delicious in this soft-textured moist loaf.
It is perfect for tea time, served with low fat spread and jam.

Serves 6

150ml/¼ pint/⅔ cup warm water
5ml/1 tsp dried yeast
pinch of sugar
10 cardamom pods
400g/14oz/3½ cups strong white flour
5ml/1 tsp salt
30ml/2 tbsp malt extract
2 ripe bananas, mashed
5ml/1 tsp sesame seeds

Cook's Tip

Make sure the bananas are really ripe, so that they impart maximum flavour to the bread. If you prefer, place the dough in one piece in a 450g/1lb loaf tin and bake for an extra 5 minutes. As well as being low in fat, bananas are a good source of potassium, therefore making an ideal nutritious, low fat snack.

NUTRITION NOTES

Per portion

Energy	299Kcals/1254kJ
Fat	1.55g
Saturated Fat	0.23g
Cholesterol	0
Fibre	2.65g

1 Put the warm water in a small bowl. Sprinkle the yeast on top. Add the sugar, mix well and leave for 10 minutes.

2 Split the cardamom pods. Remove the seeds and chop them finely.

3 Sift the flour and salt into a mixing bowl and make a well in the centre. Add the yeast mixture with the malt extract, chopped cardamom seeds and bananas.

4 Gradually incorporate the flour and mix to a soft dough, adding a little extra water if necessary. Turn the dough on to a floured surface and knead for about 5 minutes until smooth and elastic. Return to the clean bowl, cover with a damp tea towel and leave to rise for about 2 hours, until doubled in bulk.

5 Grease a baking sheet. Turn the dough on to a floured surface, knead briefly, then divide into three and shape into a plait. Place the plait on the baking sheet and cover loosely with a plastic bag (ballooning it to trap the air). Leave until well risen. Preheat the oven to 220°C/425°F/Gas 7.

6 Brush the plait lightly with water and sprinkle with the sesame seeds. Bake for 10 minutes, then lower the oven temperature to 200°C/400°F/Gas 6. Cook for 15 minutes more, or until the loaf sounds hollow when it is tapped underneath. Cool on a wire rack.

Banana Orange Loaf

For the best banana flavour and a really good, moist texture, make sure the bananas are very ripe for this cake.

Serves 8

90g/3½oz/¾ cup wholemeal plain flour
90g/3½oz/¾ cup plain flour
5ml/1 tsp baking powder
5ml/1 tsp ground mixed spice
45ml/3 tbsp flaked hazelnuts, toasted
2 large ripe bananas
1 egg
30ml/2 tbsp sunflower oil
30ml/2 tbsp clear honey
finely grated rind and juice of
1 small orange
4 orange slices, halved
10ml/2 tsp icing sugar

NUTRITION NOTES

Per portion
Energy	217Kcals/911kJ
Fat	7.59g
Saturated Fat	0.92g
Cholesterol	24.06mg
Fibre	2.46g

1 Preheat the oven to 180°C/350°F/ Gas 4.

2 Brush a 1 litre/1¾ pint/4 cup loaf tin with sunflower oil and line the base with non-stick baking paper.

3 Sift the wholemeal flour and plain flour with the baking powder and spice into a large bowl, adding any bran that is caught in the sieve. Stir the toasted hazelnuts into the dry ingredients.

4 Peel and mash the bananas. Beat together with the egg, oil, honey and the orange rind and juice. Stir evenly into the dry ingredients.

5 Spoon into the prepared tin and smooth the top. Bake for 40–45 minutes, or until firm and golden brown. Turn out and cool on a wire rack. Sprinkle the orange slices with the icing sugar and grill until golden. Use to decorate the cake.

Cook's Tip

If you plan to keep the loaf for more than two or three days, omit the orange slices, brush with honey and sprinkle with flaked hazelnuts.

Apple, Apricot and Walnut Loaf

Serve warm and store what is left in an airtight tin.

1 Preheat the oven to 180°C/350°F/ Gas 4. Line and grease a 900g/2lb loaf tin.

2 Sift the flour, baking powder and salt into a large mixing bowl, then tip the bran remaining in the sieve into the mixture. Add the margarine, sugar, eggs, orange rind and juice. Stir, then beat with a hand-held electric beater until smooth.

3 Stir in the walnuts and apricots. Peel, quarter, and core the apple, chop it roughly and add it to the mixture. Stir, then spoon into the prepared tin and level the top.

4 Bake for 1 hour, or until a skewer inserted into the centre of the loaf comes out clean. Cool in the tin for about 5 minutes, then turn the loaf out on to a wire rack and peel off the lining paper.

Serves 10–12

225g/8oz/2 cups plain wholemeal flour
5ml/1 tsp baking powder
pinch of salt
115g/4oz/½ cup sunflower margarine
175g/6oz/1 cup soft light brown sugar
2 size 2 eggs, lightly beaten
grated rind and juice of 1 orange
50g/2oz/½ cup chopped walnuts
50g/2oz/½ cup ready-to-eat dried apricots, chopped
1 large cooking apple

NUTRITION NOTES

Per portion

Energy	290Kcals/1220kJ
Fat	14.5g
Saturated Fat	2.5g
Cholesterol	43.5mg
Fibre	1.6g

Banana and Ginger Teabread

Serve this teabread in slices with low fat spread. The stem ginger adds an interesting flavour.

Serves 6–8

175g/6oz/1½ cups self-raising flour
5ml/1 tsp baking powder
40g/1½oz/3 tbsp soft margarine
50g/2oz/⅓ cup dark muscovado sugar
50g/2oz/⅓ cup drained stem
ginger, chopped
60ml/4 tbsp skimmed milk
2 ripe bananas, mashed

NUTRITION NOTES

Per portion

Energy	214Kcals/899kJ
Fat	5.16g
Saturated Fat	0.96g
Cholesterol	0.57mg
Fibre	1.59g

1 Preheat the oven to 180°C/350°F/ Gas 4. Grease and line a 450g/1lb loaf tin. Sift the flour and baking powder into a mixing bowl.

2 Rub in the margarine until the mixture resembles breadcrumbs.

3 Stir in the sugar. Add the ginger, milk and bananas and mix to a soft dough.

4 Spoon into the prepared tin and bake for 40–45 minutes, or until an inserted skewer comes out clean. Run a palette knife around the edges to loosen, then turn the teabread on to a wire rack and leave to cool.

Glazed Banana Spice Loaf

For an instant variation, omit the glaze and spread with Quark for a tea-time treat.

1 Preheat the oven to 180°C/350°F/ Gas 4. Line a 23 x 13cm/9 x 5in loaf tin with wax paper and grease.

2 With a fork, mash the banana in a bowl. Set aside.

3 With an electric mixer, cream the butter and sugar until light and fluffy. Add the eggs, one at a time, beating to blend well after each addition. Sift together the flour, salt, bicarbonate of soda, nutmeg, allspice and cloves. Add to the butter mixture and stir to combine well.

4 Add the sour cream, banana and vanilla essence and mix just enough to blend. Pour into the prepared tin.

5 Bake for 45–50 minutes, until the top springs back when touched lightly. Allow to cool in the tin for 10 minutes before turning out on to a wire rack.

6 For the glaze, combine the icing sugar and lemon juice, then stir until smooth. To glaze, set the rack over a baking sheet. Pour the glaze over the top of the bread and allow to set.

Serves 10

1 large ripe banana
115g/4oz/½ cup butter, at room temperature
175g/6oz/¾ cup granulated sugar
2 eggs, at room temperature
175g/6oz/1½ cups plain flour
5ml/1 tsp salt
5ml/1 tsp bicarbonate of soda
2.5ml/½ tsp grated nutmeg
1.5ml/¼ tsp ground allspice
1.5ml/¼ tsp ground cloves
150ml/6fl oz/¾ cup sour cream
5ml/1 tsp vanilla essence

For the glaze

175g/6oz/1 cup icing sugar
15–30ml/1–2 tbsp fresh lemon juice

NUTRITION NOTES

Per portion

Energy	362Kcals/1522kJ
Fat	14.1g
Saturated Fat	4.3g
Cholesterol	49mg
Fibre	0.8g

Orange Honey Bread

A moist and fruity bread using naturally sweet ingredients.

Serves 10

275g/10oz/2½ cups plain flour
12.5ml/2½ tsp baking powder
2.5ml/½ tsp bicarbonate of soda
2.5ml/½ tsp salt
30ml/2 tbsp margarine
350g/12oz/1 cup thin honey
1 egg, at room temperature,
lightly beaten
22.5ml/1½ tbsp grated orange rind
175ml/6fl oz/¾ cup freshly squeezed
orange juice
75g/3oz/¾ cups walnuts, chopped

NUTRITION NOTES

Per portion
Energy	300Kcals/1257kJ
Fat	11.2g
Saturated Fat	1.49g
Cholesterol	19.5mg
Fibre	1.6g

1 Preheat the oven to 175°C/325°F/ Gas 3. Sift together the flour, baking powder, bicarbonate of soda and salt.

2 Line the bottom and sides of a 23 x 13cm/9 x 5in loaf tin with wax paper and grease.

3 With an electric mixer, cream the margarine until soft. Stir in the honey until blended, then stir in the egg. Add the orange rind and stir to combine.

4 Fold the flour mixture into the honey and egg mixture in three batches, alternating with the orange juice. Stir in the walnuts.

5 Pour into the tin and bake for 60–70 minutes, or until a skewer inserted into the centre comes out clean. Allow to stand for 10 minutes before turning on to a rack to cool.

Apple-sauce Bread

Apples and spices such as cinnamon and nutmeg are a match made in heaven.

1 Preheat the oven to 180°C/350°F/ Gas 4. Line the bottom and sides of a 23 x 13cm/9 x 5in loaf tin with wax paper and grease.

2 Break the egg into a bowl and beat lightly. Stir in the baked apples, butter or margarine, and both sugars. Set aside.

3 In another bowl, sift together the flour, baking powder, bicarbonate of soda, salt, cinnamon and nutmeg. Fold the dry ingredients into the apple sauce mixture in three batches.

4 Stir in the currants or raisins and chopped pecans.

5 Pour into the prepared tin and bake for about 1 hour, or until a skewer inserted in the centre comes out clean. Let stand for 10 minutes before transferring to a cooling rack.

Serves 10

1 egg
225g/8oz/1 cup baked apples
60ml/4 tbsp butter or margarine, melted
75g/3oz/½ cup dark brown sugar, firmly packed
50g/2oz/¼ cup granulated sugar
225g/8oz/2 cups flour
10ml/2 tsp baking powder
2.5ml/½ tsp bicarbonate of soda
2.5ml/½ tsp salt
5ml/1 tsp ground cinnamon
2.5ml/½ tsp grated nutmeg
75g/3oz/½ cup currants or raisins
175g/6oz/½ cup pecans, chopped

NUTRITION NOTES

Per portion

Energy	299Kcals/1255kJ
Fat	11.2g
Saturated Fat	1.2g
Cholesterol	20mg
Fibre	1.8g

Cranberry Orange Bread

Try this classic muffin combination in a tasty teabread.

Serves 10

225g/8oz/2 cups plain flour
115g/4oz/½ cup caster sugar
15ml/1 tbsp baking powder
2.5ml/½ tsp salt
grated rind of 1 large orange
150ml/¼ pint/⅔ cup fresh orange juice
2 eggs, lightly beaten
90ml/6 tbsp butter or margarine, melted
175g/6oz/1½ cups fresh cranberries
50g/2oz/½ cup walnuts, chopped

NUTRITION NOTES

Per portion

Energy	285Kcals/1195kJ
Fat	14g
Saturated Fat	2.3g
Cholesterol	39mg
Fibre	2g

1 Preheat the oven to 180°C/350°F/ Gas 4. Line the bottom and sides of a 23 x 13cm/9 x 5in loaf tin with wax paper and grease. Sift the flour, sugar, baking powder and salt into a mixing bowl.

2 Stir the orange rind into the dry ingredients.

3 Make a well in the centre and add the orange juice, eggs and melted butter or margarine. Stir from the centre until the ingredients are blended; do not overmix.

4 Add the cranberries and walnuts and stir until blended. Transfer the batter to the prepared tin and bake for 45–50 minutes, or until a skewer inserted in the centre comes out clean.

5 Let cool in the tin for 10 minutes before transferring to a rack to cool completely. Serve thinly sliced, toasted or plain, with butter or cream cheese and jam.

Pear and Sultana Teabread

This is an ideal teabread to make when pears are plentiful – an excellent use for windfalls.

1 Preheat the oven to 180°C/350°F/ Gas 4. Grease and line a 450g/1lb loaf tin with non-stick baking paper. Put the oats in a bowl with the sugar, pour over the pear or apple juice and oil, mix well and leave to stand for 15 minutes.

2 Quarter, core and coarsely grate the pears. Add the fruit to the oat mixture with the flour, sultanas, baking powder, mixed spice and egg, then mix together thoroughly.

3 Spoon the mixture into the prepared loaf tin and level the top. Bake for 50–60 minutes or until a skewer inserted into the centre comes out clean.

4 Transfer the teabread on to a wire rack and peel off the lining paper. Leave to cool completely.

Cook's Tip
Health food shops sell concentrated pear and apple juice, ready for diluting as required.

Serves 6–8

25g/1oz/¼ cup rolled oats
50g/2oz/¼ cup light muscovado sugar
30ml/2 tbsp pear or apple juice
30ml/2 tbsp sunflower oil
1 large or 2 small pears
115g/4oz/1 cup self-raising flour
115g/4oz/¾ cup sultanas
2.5ml/½ tsp baking powder
10ml/2 tsp mixed spice
1 egg

NUTRITION NOTES
Per portion

Energy	200Kcals/814kJ
Fat	4.61g
Saturated Fat	0.79g
Cholesterol	27.5mg
Fibre	1.39g

Dried Fruit Loaf

Dried fruit is a healthy sweet treat, and delicious in this loaf.

Serves 10

425g/15oz/2½ cups mixed dried fruit,
such as currants, raisins, chopped
dried apricots and
dried cherries
300ml/½ pint/1¼ cups cold strong
black tea
175g/6oz/1 cup dark brown sugar,
firmly packed
grated rind and juice of 1 small orange
grated rind and juice of 1 lemon
1 egg, lightly beaten
200g/7oz/1¾ cups plain flour
15ml/1 tbsp baking powder
0.75ml/⅛ tsp salt

NUTRITION NOTES

Per portion

Energy	298Kcals/1252kJ
Fat	1.1g
Saturated Fat	0.2g
Cholesterol	19.2mg
Fibre	1.8g

1 In a bowl, toss together all the dried fruit, pour over the tea and leave to soak overnight.

2 Preheat the oven to 180°C/350°F/ Gas 4. Line the bottom and sides of a 23 x 13cm/9 x 5in loaf tin with wax paper and grease.

3 Strain the fruit, reserving the liquid. In a bowl, combine the sugar, orange and lemon rind and fruit.

4 Pour the orange and lemon juice into a measuring cup; if the quantity is less than 250ml/8fl oz/1 cup, make up with the soaking liquid.

5 Stir the citrus juices and egg into the dried fruit mixture.

6 In another bowl, sift together the flour, baking powder and salt. Stir into the fruit mixture until blended.

7 Transfer to the prepared tin and bake for 1¼ hours, or until a skewer inserted in the centre comes out clean. Allow to stand for 10 minutes before turning out.

Date and Nut Malt Loaf

A moist loaf – perfect for packed lunches.

1 Sift the flours and salt into a large bowl, adding any bran from the sieve. Stir in the sugar and yeast.

2 Put the butter or margarine in a small pan with the treacle and malt extract. Stir over a low heat until melted. Leave to cool, then combine with the milk.

3 Stir the liquid into the dry ingredients and knead thoroughly for 15 minutes until the dough is elastic. (If you have a dough blade on your food processor, follow the manufacturer's instructions for timings.)

4 Knead in the fruits and nuts. Transfer the dough to an oiled bowl, cover with the clear film, and leave in a warm place for about 1½ hours, until the dough has doubled in size.

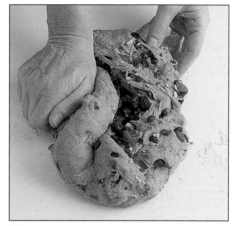

5 Grease two 450g/1lb loaf tins. Knock back the dough and knead lightly. Divide in half, form into loaves and place in the tins. Cover and leave in a warm place for about 30 minutes, until risen. Meanwhile, preheat the oven to 190°C/375°F/Gas 5.

6 Bake for 35–40 minutes, until well risen and sounding hollow when tapped underneath. Cool on a wire rack. Brush with honey while warm.

Makes two 450g/1lb loaves

300g/11oz/2 cups strong plain flour
275g/10oz/2 cups strong plain wholemeal flour
5ml/1 tsp salt
75g/3oz/6 tbsp soft brown sugar
15ml/1 tsp easy-blend dried yeast
50g/2oz/¼ tbsp butter or margarine
15ml/1 tbsp black treacle
60ml/4 tbsp malt extract
scant 250ml/8fl oz/1 cup tepid milk
115g/4oz/½ cup chopped dates
75g/3oz/½ cup sultanas
75g/3oz/½ cup raisins
50g/2oz/½ cup chopped nuts
30ml/2 tbsp clear honey, to glaze

NUTRITION NOTES

Per portion

Energy	216Kcals/907kJ
Fat	5.57g
Saturated Fat	2.46g
Cholesterol	9.45mg
Fibre	2.8g

Malt Loaf

This is a rich and sticky loaf. If it lasts long enough to go stale, try toasting it for a delicious tea-time treat.

Serves 8

150ml/¼ pint/⅔ cup warm skimmed milk
5ml/1 tsp dried yeast
pinch of caster sugar
350g/12oz/3 cups plain flour
1.5ml/½ tsp salt
30ml/2 tbsp light muscovado sugar
175g/6oz/generous 1 cup sultanas
15ml/1 tbsp sunflower oil
45ml/3 tbsp malt extract

For the glaze

30ml/2 tbsp caster sugar
30ml/2 tbsp water

Cook's Tip

To make buns, divide the dough into 10 pieces, shape into rounds, leave to rise, then bake for about 15–20 minutes. Brush with the glaze while still hot.

NUTRITION NOTES

Per portion

Energy	279Kcals/1171kJ
Fat	2.06g
Saturated Fat	0.33g
Cholesterol	0.38mg
Fibre	1.79g

1 Place the warm milk in a bowl. Sprinkle the yeast on top and add the sugar. Leave for 30 minutes until frothy. Stir the flour and salt into a mixing bowl, stir in the muscovado sugar and sultanas, and make a well in the centre.

2 Add the yeast mixture with the oil and malt extract. Gradually incorporate the flour and mix to a soft dough, adding a little extra milk if necessary.

3 Turn on to a floured surface and knead for about 5 minutes until smooth and elastic. Grease a 450g/1lb loaf tin.

4 Shape the dough and place it in the prepared loaf tin. Cover with a damp tea towel and leave in a warm place for about 1–2 hours until the dough is well risen. Preheat the oven to 190°C/375°F/Gas 5.

5 Bake the loaf for 30–35 minutes, or until it sounds hollow when it is tapped underneath.

6 Meanwhile, prepare the glaze by dissolving the sugar in the water in a small pan. Bring to the boil, stirring, then lower the heat and simmer for 1 minute. Place the loaf on a wire rack and brush with the glaze while still hot. Leave the loaf to cool before serving.

Lemon Walnut Bread

This is a light and tangy teabread.

Serves 10

115g/40z/½ cup butter or margarine, at
room temperature
115g/4oz/½ cup caster sugar
2 eggs, at room temperature, separated
grated rind of 2 lemons
30ml/2 tbsp fresh lemon juice
175g/6oz/1½ cups self-raising flour
10ml/2 tsp baking powder
120ml/4fl oz/½ cup milk
175g/6oz/½ cup walnuts, chopped
0.75ml/⅛ tsp salt

NUTRITION NOTES

Per portion

Energy	229Kcals/962kJ
Fat	11.1g
Saturated Fat	1.77g
Cholesterol	39.1mg
Fibre	1g

1 Preheat the oven to 180°C/350°F/ Gas 4. Line the bottom and sides of a 23 x 13cm/9 x 5in loaf tin with wax paper and grease.

2 With an electric mixer, cream the butter or margarine with the sugar until light and fluffy.

3 Beat the egg yolks into the creamed butter and sugar.

4 Add the lemon rind and juice and stir until blended. Set aside.

5 In another bowl, sift together the flour and baking powder, three times. Fold into the butter mixture in three batches, alternating with the milk. Fold in the chopped walnuts and set the mixture aside.

6 Beat the egg whites and salt until stiff peaks form. Fold a large dollop of the egg whites into the walnut mixture to lighten it. Fold in the remaining egg whites carefully until just blended.

7 Pour the batter into the prepared tin and bake for 45–50 minutes, or until a skewer inserted in the centre of the loaf comes out clean. Let stand for 5 minutes before turning on to a rack to cool completely.

Apricot Nut Loaf

An excellent high fibre fruit and nut combination.

1 Preheat the oven to 180°C/350°F/ Gas 4. Line the bottom and sides of a 23 x 13cm/9 x 5in loaf tin with wax paper and grease.

2 Place the apricots in a bowl and add lukewarm water to cover. Allow to stand for 30 minutes.

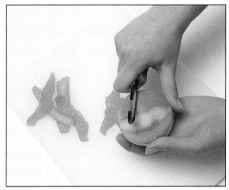

3 With a vegetable peeler, remove the orange rind, leaving the pith.

4 With a sharp knife, finely chop the orange rind strips.

5 Drain the apricots and chop coarsely. Place in a bowl with the orange rind and raisins. Set aside.

6 Squeeze the peeled orange. Measure the juice and add enough hot water to make 175ml/6fl oz/¾ cup liquid.

7 Pour the orange juice mixture over the apricot mixture. Stir in the sugar, oil and eggs. Set aside.

8 In another bowl, sift together the flour, baking powder, salt and bicarbonate of soda. Fold the flour mixture into the apricot mixture in three batches.

9 Stir in the walnuts. Spoon the batter into the prepared tin and bake for about 55–60 minutes, or until a skewer inserted in the centre of the loaf comes out clean. If the loaf browns too quickly, protect the top with foil. Cool in the tin for 10 minutes before transferring to a rack to cool completely.

Serves 10

175g/6oz/¾ cup dried apricots
1 large orange
75g/3oz/½ cup raisins
150g/5oz/⅔ cups caster sugar
90ml/3fl oz/⅓ cup oil
2 eggs, lightly beaten
250g/9oz/2¼ cups plain flour
10ml/2 tsp baking powder
2.5ml/½ tsp salt
5ml/1 tsp bicarbonate soda
50g/2oz/½ cup walnuts, chopped

NUTRITION NOTES
Per portion

Energy	324Kcals/1365kJ
Fat	11.2g
Saturated Fat	1.5g
Cholesterol	38mg
Fibre	2.5g

Date-nut Bread

A little brandy gives this teabread an extra rich flavour.

Serves 10

150g/50z/1 cup pitted dates, chopped
175ml/6fl oz/¾ cup boiling water
60ml/4 tbsp unsalted butter, at room
temperature
40g/1½oz/¼ cup dark brown sugar,
firmly packed
50g/2oz/¼ caster sugar
1 egg, at room temperature
30ml/2 tbsp brandy
165g/5½oz/1⅓ cups plain flour
10ml/2 tsp baking powder
2.5ml/½ tsp salt
generous 2.5ml/½ tsp/¾ tsp freshly
grated nutmeg
175g/3oz/¾ cup pecans, coarsely chopped

NUTRITION NOTES

Per portion

Energy	258Kcals/1077kJ
Fat	13.8g
Saturated Fat	1.1g
Cholesterol	20mg
Fibre	1.3g

1 Place the dates in a bowl and pour over the boiling water. Set aside to cool to lukewarm.

2 Preheat the oven to 180°C/350°F/ Gas 4. Line the bottom and sides of a 23 x 13cm/9 x 5in loaf tin with wax paper and grease.

3 With an electric mixer, cream the butter and sugars until they are light and fluffy. Beat in the egg and brandy, then set aside.

4 Sift the flour, baking powder, salt and nutmeg together, three times.

5 Fold the dry ingredients into the sugar mixture in three batches, alternating with the dates and water.

6 Fold in the pecans. Pour the batter into the prepared tin and bake for 45–50 minutes, or until a skewer inserted in the centre comes out clean. Cool in the pan for 10 minutes before transferring to a rack to cool completely.

Prune Bread

A slightly spicy bread that tastes good with savoury spreads.

1 Simmer the prunes in water to cover until soft, or soak overnight. Drain, reserving 50ml/2fl oz/¼ cup of the soaking liquid. Pit and chop the prunes.

2 Combine the yeast and the reserved prune liquid, stir, and leave for 15 minutes to dissolve.

3 In a large bowl, stir together the flours, bicarbonate of soda, salt and pepper. Make a well in the centre.

4 Add the chopped prunes, butter and buttermilk. Pour in the yeast mixture. With a wooden spoon, stir from the centre, incorporating more flour with each turn, to obtain a rough dough.

5 Transfer to a floured surface and knead until smooth and elastic. Return to the clean bowl, cover with a plastic bag, and leave to rise in a warm place until doubled in volume, for about 1½ hours. Grease a baking sheet.

6 Punch down the dough with your fist, then knead in the walnuts.

7 Shape the dough into a long, cylindrical loaf. Place on the baking sheet, cover loosely, and leave to rise in a warm place for 45 minutes.

8 Preheat the oven to 220°C/425°F/ Gas 7. With a sharp knife, score the top deeply. Brush with milk and bake for 15 minutes. Lower the heat to 190°C/ 375°F/Gas 5 and bake for about 35 minutes more, until the bottom sounds hollow when tapped. Cool on a rack.

Serves 10

225g/8oz/1 cup dried prunes
10ml/2 tsp active dry yeast
50g/2oz/½ cup wholewheat flour
257–350g/10–12oz/2½–3 cups
plain flour
2.5ml/½ tsp bicarbonate of soda
5ml/1 tsp salt
5ml/1 tsp freshly ground black pepper
30ml/2 tbsp butter, at room temperature
175ml/6fl oz/¾ cup buttermilk
175g/6oz/½ cup walnuts, chopped
milk, for glazing

NUTRITION NOTES

Per portion

Energy	262Kcals/1104kJ
Fat	8.4g
Saturated Fat	1.1g
Cholesterol	1mg
Fibre	2.1g

Swedish Sultana Bread

A lightly sweetened fruit bread that is delicious served warm. It is also excellent toasted and topped with low fat spread.

Serves 8–10

150ml/¼ pint/⅔ cup warm water
5ml/1 tsp dried yeast
15ml/1 tbsp clear honey
225g/8oz/2 cups wholemeal flour
225g/8oz/2 cups strong white flour
5ml/1 tsp salt
115g/4oz/⅔ cup sultanas
50g/2oz/½ cup walnuts, finely chopped
175ml/6fl oz/¾ cups warm skimmed milk, plus extra for glazing

Cook's Tip
To make Apple and Hazelnut Bread, replace the sultanas with two chopped eating apples and use chopped toasted hazelnuts instead of the walnuts. Add 5ml/1 tsp ground cinnamon with the flour.

NUTRITION NOTES
Per portion
Energy	273Kcals/1145kJ
Fat	4.86g
Saturated Fat	0.57g
Cholesterol	0.39mg
Fibre	3.83g

1 Put the water in a small jug. Sprinkle the yeast on top. Add a few drops of the honey to help activate the yeast, mix well and leave to stand for 10 minutes.

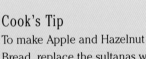

2 Put the flours in a mixing bowl, with the salt and sultanas. Set aside 15ml/1 tbsp of the walnuts and add the rest to the bowl. Mix together lightly and make a well in the centre.

3 Add the yeast and honey mixture to the flour mixture with the milk and remaining honey. Gradually incorporate the flour, mixing to a soft dough; add a little extra water if the dough feels too dry to work with.

4 Turn the dough on to a floured surface and knead for 5 minutes until smooth and elastic. Return to the clean bowl, cover with a damp tea towel and leave in a warm place to rise for about 2 hours until doubled in bulk. Grease a baking sheet.

5 Turn the dough on to a floured surface and form into a 28cm/11in long sausage shape. Place on the baking sheet. Make some diagonal cuts down the whole length of the loaf.

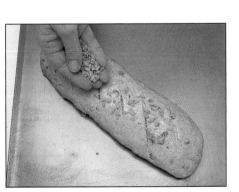

6 Brush the loaf with milk, sprinkle with the reserved walnuts and leave to rise for about 40 minutes. Preheat the oven to 220°C/425°F/Gas 7. Bake for 10 minutes. Lower the temperature to 200°C/400°F/Gas 6 and bake for about 20 minutes more, or until the loaf sounds hollow when tapped.

Raisin Bread

Spice, brandy and dried fruit make a good flavour combination.

Serves 20
10ml/2 tsp active dry yeast
475ml/16fl oz/2 cups lukewarm milk
175g/6oz/1 cup raisins
65g/2½oz/½ cup currants
15ml/1 tbsp sherry or brandy
2.5ml/½ tsp grated nutmeg
grated rind of 1 large orange
75g/3oz/⅓ cup caster sugar
15ml/1 tbsp salt
120ml/8 tbsp butter, melted
500–675g/1½–1½lb/5–6 cups
plain flour
1 egg beaten with 15ml/1 tbsp cream,
for glazing

NUTRITION NOTES
Per portion
Energy   235Kcals/994kJ
Fat   5.9g
Saturated Fat   1.2g
Cholesterol   11mg
Fibre   1.4g

1 Stir together the yeast and 120ml/4fl oz/½ cup of the milk and let stand for 15 minutes to dissolve.

2 Mix the raisins, currants, sherry or brandy, nutmeg and orange rind together and set aside.

3 In another bowl, mix the remaining milk, sugar, salt and 60ml/4 tbsp of the butter. Add the yeast mixture. With a wooden spoon, stir in 225–270g/8–10oz/2–3 cups flour, 115g/4oz/1 cup at a time, until blended. Add more flour for a stiff dough.

4 Transfer to a floured surface and knead until smooth and elastic. Place in a greased bowl, cover, and leave to rise in a warm place until doubled in volume, for about 2½ hours.

5 Punch down the dough, return to the bowl, cover, and leave to rise in a warm place for about 30 minutes.

6 Grease two 23 x 13cm/9 x 5in bread tins. Divide the dough in half and roll each half into a rectangle about 50 x 18cm/20 x 7in.

7 Brush the rectangles with the remaining melted butter. Sprinkle over the raising mixture, then roll up tightly from the short end, tucking in the ends slightly as you roll. Place in the prepared tins, cover and leave to rise until almost doubled in volume.

8 Preheat the oven to 200°C/400°F/Gas 6. Brush the top of the loaves with the glaze. Bake for 20 minutes. Lower the heat to 180°C/350°F/Gas 4 and bake for 25–30 minutes more, or until golden. Cool on racks.

Sweet Potato and Raisin Bread

The natural sweetness of sweet potato is used in this healthy loaf.

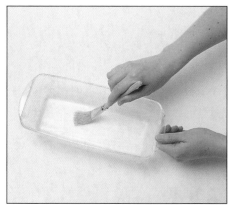

1 Preheat the oven to 180°C/350°F/ Gas 4. Grease a 23 x 13cm/9 x 5in loaf tin.

2 Sift the flour, baking powder, salt, cinnamon and nutmeg into a small bowl. Set aside.

3 With an electric mixer, beat the mashed sweet potatoes with the brown sugar, butter or margarine and eggs until well mixed.

4 Add the flour mixture and the raisins. Stir with a wooden spoon until the flour is just mixed in.

5 Transfer the batter to the prepared tin. Bake for 1–1¼ hours, or until a skewer inserted in the centre comes out clean.

6 Cool in the pan on a wire rack for 15 minutes, then turn the bread on to the wire rack and cool completely.

Serves 10

225–275g/8–10oz/2½ cups plain flour
10ml/2 tsp baking powder
2.5ml/½ tsp salt
5ml/1 tsp ground cinnamon
2.5ml/½ tsp grated nutmeg
450g/1lb/2 cups mashed cooked sweet potatoes
75g/3oz/½ cup light brown sugar, firmly packed
115g/4oz/½ cup butter or margarine, melted and cooled
3 eggs, beaten
75g/3oz/½ cup raisins

NUTRITION NOTES

Per portion

Energy	338Kcals/1420kJ
Fat	11.6g
Saturated Fat	2.4g
Cholesterol	59mg
Fibre	2.4g

Cardamom and Saffron Tealoaf

An aromatic sweet bread ideal for afternoon tea or lightly toasted for breakfast. Using the sachets of fast-action or easy-blend yeasts make bread-making so simple.

Serves 20

good pinch of saffron strands
750ml/1¼ pints/3 cups lukewarm milk
25g/1oz/2 tbsp butter
1kg/2lb/8 cups strong·plain flour
10ml/2 tsp fast-action yeast
30g/1½oz caster sugar
6 cardamom pods, split open and
seeds extracted
115g/4oz/⅔ cup raisins
30ml/2 tbsp clear honey
1 egg, beaten

NUTRITION NOTES

Per portion

Energy	226Kcals/952kJ
Fat	2.1g
Saturated Fat	0.4g
Cholesterol	10mg
Fibre	1.7g

1 Crush the saffron into a cup containing a little of the warm milk and leave to infuse for 5 minutes.

2 Rub the butter into the flour, then mix in the yeast, sugar and cardamom seeds (these may need rubbing to separate them). Stir in the raisins.

3 Beat the remaining·milk with the honey and egg, then mix this into the flour along with the saffron milk and strands, stirring well until a firm dough is formed. You may not need all the milk; it depends on the flour.

4 Turn out the dough and knead it on a lightly floured board for about 5 minutes until smooth.

5 Return the dough to the mixing bowl, cover with oiled clear film and leave in a warm place until doubled in size. This could take between 1–3 hours. Grease a 1kg/2lb loaf tin. Turn the dough out on to a floured board again, punch it down, knead for three minutes, then shape it into a fat roll and fit it into the greased loaf tin.

6 Cover with a sheet of lightly oiled clear film and stand in a warm place until the dough begins to rise again. Preheat the oven to 200°C/400°F/Gas 6. Bake the loaf for 25 minutes until golden brown and firm on top. Turn out of the tin and as it cools, brush the top with honey. Slice when cold and spread·with the butter. It is also good lightly toasted.

Sweet Sesame Loaf

Toasted sesame seeds add a lovely nutty flavour to this loaf.

1 Preheat the oven to 180°C/350°F/ Gas 4. Line a 25 x 15cm/10 x 6in baking tin, or two small loaf tins, with wax paper and grease.

2 Reserve 30ml/2 tbsp of the sesame seeds. Spread the rest on a baking sheet and bake until lightly toasted, for about 10 minutes. Sift the flour, baking powder and salt into a bowl.

5 Pour into the pan and sprinkle over the reserved sesame seeds.

6 Bake for about 1 hour, or until a skewer inserted in the centre comes out clean. Cool in the pan for 10 minutes before turning out.

Serves 10

5oz/12 tbsp/⅔ cup sesame seeds
225g/8oz/2 cups plain flour
12.5ml/2½ tsp baking powder
5ml/1 tsp salt
60ml/4 tbsp butter or margarine, at room temperature
150g/5oz/⅔ cup caster sugar
2 eggs, at room temperature
grated rind of 1 lemon
350ml/12fl oz/1½ cups milk

NUTRITION NOTES

Per portion

Energy	133Kcals/562kJ
Fat	5.1g
Saturated Fat	0.9g
Cholesterol	20mg
Fibre	0.7g

3 Stir in the toasted sesame seeds and set aside. With an electric mixer, cream the butter or margarine and sugar together until light and fluffy. Beat in the eggs, then stir in the lemon rind and milk.

4 Pour the milk mixture over the dry ingredients and fold in with a large metal spoon until just blended.

Greek Easter Bread

In Greece, Easter celebrations are very important, and involve much preparation in the kitchen. This bread is sold in all the bakers' shops, and is also made at home. It is traditionally decorated with red dyed eggs.

Serves 10

25g/1oz fresh yeast
120ml/4fl oz/½ cup warm milk
675g/1½lb/6 cups strong plain flour
2 eggs, beaten
2.5ml/½ tsp caraway seeds
15ml/1 tbsp caster sugar
15ml/1 tbsp brandy
50g/2oz/4 tbsp butter, melted
1 egg white, beaten
50g/2oz/½ cup split almonds
2–3 hard-boiled eggs, dyed red

NUTRITION NOTES

Per portion

Energy	344Kcals/1453kJ
Fat	10.1g
Saturated Fat	3.6g
Cholesterol	89mg
Fibre	2.5g

1 Crumble the yeast into a bowl. Mix with 15-30ml/½–1fl oz/1–2 tbsp of warm water, until softened. Add the milk and 115g/4oz/1 cup of the flour and mix to a creamy consistency. Cover with a cloth, and leave in a warm place to rise for 1 hour.

2 Sift the remaining flour into a large bowl and make a well in the centre. Pour the risen yeast into the well, and draw in a little of the flour from the sides. Add the eggs, caraway seeds, sugar and brandy. Incorporate the remaining flour until the mixture begins to form a dough.

3 Mix in the melted butter. Turn on to a floured surface and knead for about 10 minutes, until the dough becomes smooth. Return to the bowl and cover with a tea towel. Leave in a warm place for 3 hours.

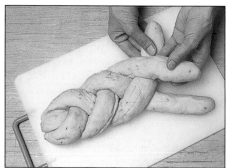

4 Preheat the oven to 180°C/350°F/ Gas 4. Knock back the dough, turn on to a floured surface and knead for a minute or two. Divide the dough into three, and roll each piece into a long sausage shape. Make a plait as shown above and place the loaf on a greased baking sheet.

5 Tuck the ends under, brush with the egg white and decorate with the split almonds. Bake for about 1 hour, until the loaf sounds hollow when tapped on the bottom. Cool on a wire rack. Serve decorated with the hard-boiled eggs.

Orange Wheat Loaf

Perfect just with butter as a breakfast bread or teabread and lovely for banana sandwiches.

1 Sift the flour into a large bowl and return any wheat flakes from the sieve. Add the salt and rub in the butter lightly with your fingertips.

2 Stir in the sugar, yeast and orange rind. Pour the orange juice into a measuring jug and make up to 200ml/ 7fl oz/⅞ cup with hot water (the liquid should not be more than hand hot).

3 Stir the liquid into the flour and mix to a soft ball of dough. Knead the dough gently on a lightly floured surface until quite smooth.

4 Place the dough in a greased 450g/ 1lb loaf tin and leave in a warm place until nearly doubled in size. Preheat the oven to 220°C/425°F/Gas 7.

5 Bake the bread for 30–35 minutes, or until it sounds hollow when you tap the underneath. Tip out of the tin and cool on a wire rack.

Makes one 450g/1lb loaf

275g/10 oz/2¼ cups wholemeal plain flour
2.5ml/½ tsp salt
50g/2 oz/4 tbsp butter
25g/1 oz/2 tbsp soft light brown sugar
½ sachet easy-blend dried yeast
grated rind and juice of ½ orange

NUTRITION NOTES

Per portion

Energy	144Kcals/607kJ
Fat	3.32g
Saturated Fat	1.82g
Cholesterol	7.19mg
Fibre	3.24g

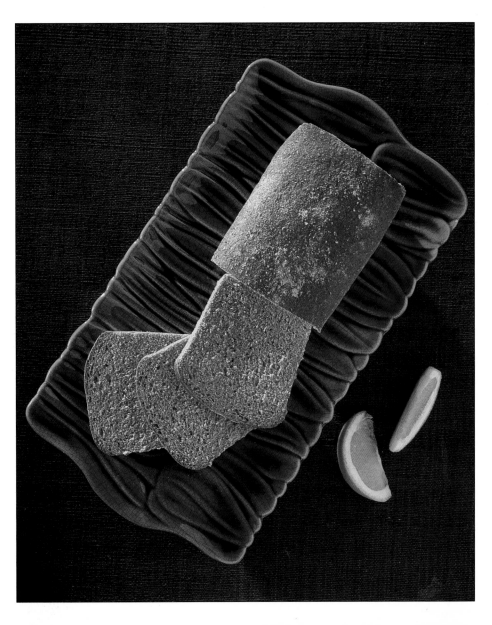

Savoury Bakes

Savoury bakes such as pizzas, soufflés, and tartlets are irresistible served warm or piping hot. As an extra bonus, popovers, parcels and scones are also very quick to make!

Smoked Salmon Pizzettes

Mini pizzas topped with smoked salmon, crème fraîche and lumpfish roe make
an extra special party canapé.

Makes 10–12

150g/5oz packet of pizza dough mix
15ml/1 tbsp snipped
fresh chives
15ml/1 tbsp olive oil
75–115g/3–4oz smoked salmon,
cut into strips
60ml/4 tbsp crème fraîche
30ml/2 tbsp black lumpfish roe
chives, to garnish

NUTRITION NOTES

Per portion
Energy   126Kcals/532kJ
Fat   2.9g
Saturated Fat   0.8g
Cholesterol   37mg
Fibre   0.9g

1 Preheat the oven to 200°C/400°F/
Gas 6. Grease two baking sheets.
Knead the dough gently, adding the
chives until evenly mixed.

2 Roll out the dough on a lightly floured
surface to about 3mm/⅛in thick.
Using a 7.5cm/3in plain round cutter,
stamp out 10–12 rounds.

3 Place the bases well apart on the two
baking sheets, prick all over with a
fork, then brush with the oil. Bake for
10–15 minutes until crisp and golden.

4 Arrange the smoked salmon on top,
then spoon on the crème fraîche.
Spoon a tiny amount of lumpfish roe in
the centre and garnish with chives.
Serve immediately.

Calzone

Cut into this folded pizza to reveal a deliciously tempting filling.

1 To make the dough, sift the flour and
salt into a bowl and stir in the yeast.
Stir in just enough warm water to mix a
soft dough.

2 Knead for 5 minutes until smooth.
Cover and leave in a warm place for
about 1 hour, or until doubled in size.

3 Meanwhile, to make the filling, heat
the oil and sauté the onion and
courgettes for 3–4 minutes. Remove
from the heat and add the tomatoes,
cheese, oregano and seasoning.

4 Preheat the oven to 220°C/425°F/
Gas 7. Knead the dough lightly and
divide into four. Roll out each piece on a
lightly floured surface to a 20cm/8in
round and place a quarter of the filling on
one half of each round.

5 Brush the edges with milk and fold
over to enclose the filling. Press
firmly to enclose. Brush with milk.

6 Bake on an oiled baking sheet for
15–20 minutes. Serve hot or cold.

Serves 4
450g/1lb/4 cups plain flour
pinch of salt
10ml/2 tsp easy-blend yeast
about 350ml/12fl oz/1½ cups
warm water

For the filling
5ml/1 tsp olive oil
1 medium red onion, thinly sliced
3 medium courgettes, sliced
2 large tomatoes, diced
150g/5oz mozzarella cheese, diced
15ml/1 tbsp chopped fresh oregano
salt and freshly ground black pepper
skimmed milk, to glaze

NUTRITION NOTES

Per portion
Energy	544Kcals/2885kJ
Fat	10.93g
Saturated Fat	5.49g
Cholesterol	24.42mg
Fibre	5.09g

Fresh Herb Pizza

Cut this pizza into thin wedges and serve as part of a mixed antipasti.

Serves 8

115g/4oz mixed fresh herbs, such as
parsley, basil and oregano
3 garlic cloves, crushed
120ml/4fl oz/½ cup double cream
1 pizza base, 25–30cm/
10–12in diameter
15ml/1 tbsp garlic oil
115g/4oz/1 cup Pecorino cheese, grated
salt and freshly ground black pepper

NUTRITION NOTES

Per portion

Energy	219Kcals/913kJ
Fat	8.1g
Saturated Fat	3.4g
Cholesterol	27mg
Fibre	1g

1 Preheat the oven to 220°C/425°F/
Gas 7. Chop the herbs, using a food
processor if you have one.

2 In a bowl, mix together the herbs,
garlic, cream and seasoning.

3 Brush the pizza base with the garlic
oil, then spread over the herb and
garlic mixture.

4 Sprinkle over the Pecorino cheese.
Bake for 15–20 minutes until crisp
and golden and the topping is still moist.
Cut into thin wedges to serve.

Mini Pizzas

For a quick supper, try these delicious little pizzas made with fresh and sun-dried tomatoes.

1 Preheat the oven to 200°C/400°F/ Gas 6. Make up the pizza base following the instructions on the side of the packet.

4 Top with the tomato slices and crumble over the goat's cheese. Bake for 10–15 minutes. Sprinkle with the fresh basil and serve at once.

Makes 4
150g/5oz packet of pizza dough mix
8 halves sun-dried tomatoes in olive oil, drained
50g/2oz/½ cup black olives, pitted
225g/8oz/1 large ripe tomato, sliced
50g/2oz/¼ cup goat's cheese
30ml/2 tbsp fresh basil leaves

NUTRITION NOTES
Per portion

Energy	326Kcals/1369kJ
Fat	11.3g
Saturated Fat	2.8g
Cholesterol	34mg
Fibre	2.8g

2 Divide the dough into four and roll each piece out to a 13cm/5in round. Place on two lightly oiled baking sheets.

3 Place the sun-dried tomatoes and olives in a blender or food processor and blend until smooth. Spread the mixture evenly over the pizza bases.

Cook's Tip
You could use loose sun-dried tomatoes (preserved without oil) instead. Leave in a bowl of warm water for 10–15 minutes to soften, drain and blend with the olives.

Spinach and Feta Triangles

Feta is a medium fat cheese and has a tangy flavour.

Serves 20

30ml/2 tbsp olive oil
2 shallots, finely chopped
450g/1lb/3 cups frozen spinach, thawed
115g/4oz/½ cup feta cheese, crumbled
25g/1oz/⅓ cup walnut pieces, chopped
1.5ml/¼ tsp grated nutmeg
4 large or 8 small sheets filo pastry
50g/2oz/½ cup butter or margarine, melted
salt and freshly ground black pepper

Cook's Tip

For an alternative filling, omit the spinach and shallots. Use 350g/12oz/1½ cups crumbled goat's cheese, instead of the feta cheese, and 50g/2oz/½ cup toasted pine nuts instead of the walnuts. Mix the cheese with the olive oil and 15ml/1 tbsp chopped fresh basil. Assemble as above.

NUTRITION NOTES

Per portion

Energy	105Kcals/434J
Fat	9g
Saturated Fat	2g
Cholesterol	4mg
Fibre	0.6g

1 Preheat the oven to 200°C/400°F/ Gas 6.

2 Heat the olive oil in a skillet. Add the shallots and cook until softened, for about 5 minutes.

3 A handful at a time, squeeze all the liquid out of the spinach. Add the spinach to the shallots. Increase the heat to high and cook, stirring until all the excess moisture has evaporated, for about 5 minutes.

4 Transfer the spinach mixture to a bowl. Cool. Stir in the feta and walnuts. Season with nutmeg, salt and pepper.

5 Lay a filo sheet on a flat surface. (Keep the remaining filo covered with a damp cloth to prevent it drying out.) Brush with some of the butter or margarine. Lay a second filo sheet on top of the first. With scissors, cut the layered filo pastry lengthways into 7.5cm/3in wide strips.

6 Place 15ml/1tbsp of the spinach mixture at the end of one strip of filo pastry.

7 Fold a bottom corner of the pastry over the filling to form a triangle, then continue folding over the pastry strip to the other end. Fill and shape the triangles until all the ingredients are used.

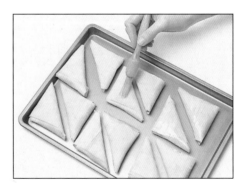

8 Set the triangles on baking sheets and brush with butter. Bake the filo triangles until they are crispy and golden brown, for about 10 minutes. Serve hot.

Salmon Parcels

Serve these little savoury parcels just as they are for a snack, or with a pool of fresh tomato sauce for a special starter.

Makes 12

90g/3½oz can red or pink salmon
15ml/1 tbsp chopped fresh coriander
4 spring onions, finely chopped
4 sheets filo pastry
sunflower oil, for brushing
spring onions and salad leaves,
to serve

NUTRITION NOTES

Per portion
Energy	25Kcals/107kJ
Fat	1.16g
Saturated Fat	0.23g
Cholesterol	2.55mg
Fibre	0.05g

1 Preheat the oven to 200°C/400°F/ Gas 6. Lightly oil a baking sheet. Drain the salmon, discarding any skin and bones, then place in a bowl.

2 Flake the salmon with a fork and then mix with the fresh coriander and spring onions.

3 Place a single sheet of filo pastry on a work surface and brush lightly with oil. Then place another sheet on top. Cut into six squares, about 10cm/4in. Repeat with the remaining pastry, to make 12 squares.

4 Place a spoonful of the salmon mixture on to each square. Brush the edges of the pastry with oil, then draw together as shown above, pressing to seal. Place the pastries on a baking sheet and bake for 12–15 minutes, until golden. Serve warm, with spring onions and salad leaves.

Cook's Tip

When you are using filo pastry, it is important to prevent it drying out; cover any you are not using with a tea towel or clear film.

Tomato Cheese Tarts

These crisp little tartlets are easier to make than they look. They are best eaten fresh from the oven.

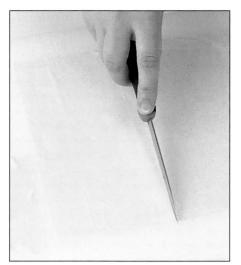

Serves 4

2 sheets filo pastry
1 egg white
115g/4oz/½ cup skimmed
milk soft cheese
handful of fresh basil leaves
3 small tomatoes, sliced
salt and freshly ground black pepper

NUTRITION NOTES
Per portion

Energy	50Kcals/210kJ
Fat	0.33g
Saturated Fat	0.05g
Cholesterol	0.29mg
Fibre	0.25g

1 Preheat the oven to 200°C/400°F/ Gas 6. Brush the sheets of filo pastry lightly with egg white and cut into sixteen 10cm/4in squares.

3 Arrange tomatoes on the tarts, add seasoning and bake for 10–12 minutes, until golden. Serve warm.

2 Layer the squares in twos, in eight patty tins. Spoon the cheese into the pastry cases. Season with black pepper and top with basil leaves.

Red Pepper and Watercress Filo Parcels

Peppery watercress combines well with sweet red pepper in these crisp little parcels.

Makes 8
3 red peppers
175g/6oz/1 bunch watercress
225g/8oz/1 cup ricotta cheese
50g/2oz/¼ cup blanched almonds,
toasted and chopped
8 sheets filo pastry
30ml/2 tbsp olive oil
salt and freshly ground black pepper

NUTRITION NOTES
Per portion

Energy	168Kcals/699kJ
Fat	10.2g
Saturated Fat	2.7g
Cholesterol	14mg
Fibre	1.7g

1 Preheat the oven to 190°C/375°F/ Gas 5. Place the peppers under a hot grill until blistered and charred. Place in a plastic bag. When cool enough to handle, peel, seed and pat dry on kitchen paper.

2 Place the peppers and watercress in a food processor and blend until coarsely chopped. Spoon into a bowl.

3 Mix in the ricotta and almonds, and season to taste.

4 Working with one sheet of filo pastry at a time, cut out two 8cm/7in and two 5cm/2in squares from each sheet. Brush one large square with a little olive oil and place a second large square at an angle of 90 degrees to form a star shape.

5 Place one of the small squares in the centre of the star shape, brush lightly with oil and top with a second small squares.

6 Top with ⅛ of the red pepper mixture. Bring the edges together to form a purse shape and twist to seal. Place on a lightly greased baking sheet and cook for 25–30 minutes until golden.

Filo Clam Puffs

Mouthwatering bite-size parcels of seafood.

Makes 54

9 sheets filo pastry, each about
30 x 46cm/12 x 18in
350g/12oz/1½ cups skimmed
milk soft cheese
1 egg, beaten
140g/5oz/1 cup coarsely chopped
steamed clams or well drained
canned clams
25g/1oz/⅓ cups chopped spring onions
30ml/2 tbsp chopped fresh dill
a few drops of hot pepper sauce
225–350g/8–12oz/¾–1 cup butter or
margarine, melted
salt and freshly ground black pepper

NUTRITION NOTES

Per portion

Energy	51Kcals/213kJ
Fat	3.4g
Saturated Fat	0.9g
Cholesterol	5mg
Fibre	0

1 Preheat the oven to 200°C/400°F/ Gas 6. Stack the sheets of filo pastry and cover with a sheet of clear film.

2 Combine the soft cheese, egg, clams, spring onions, dill, pepper sauce, and some salt and pepper in a bowl. Mix thoroughly.

3 Lay one sheet of filo pastry on the work surface and brush it lightly and evenly with melted butter. Lay another sheet of filo pastry neatly on top and brush it with butter. Cover with a third sheet of filo pastry and brush with butter.

4 Spoon about one-third of the clam mixture in a line along one side of the stacked filo pastry, about 2.5cm/1in in from the edge.

5 Fold the nearest long filo pastry edge over the clam filling and continue rolling up. Cut the roll across in half and put the two halves on a buttered baking sheet. Brush the rolls with melted butter.

6 Make two more rolls in the same way and put the halves on the baking sheet. Brush them all with melted butter. Bake until golden brown and crisp, for about 20 minutes. Using scissors, cut the rolls across into bite-size pieces. Serve as soon as possible, as a starter.

Spinach and Cheese Pie

Using low fat cottage cheese cuts calories with this delicious pie.

1 Preheat the oven to 190°C/375°F/ Gas 5.

2 Stack handfuls of spinach leaves, roll them loosely, and cut across the leaves into thin ribbons. Heat the oil in a large saucepan. Add the onion and cook until softened, for about 5 minutes.

3 Add the spinach and oregano and cook for about 5 minutes over a high heat until most of the liquid from the spinach evaporates, stirring frequently. Remove from the heat and let cool. Break the eggs into a bowl and beat. Stir in the cottage cheese and Parmesan cheese and season generously with nutmeg, salt and pepper. Stir in the spinach mixture.

4 Brush a 33 x 23cm/13 x 9in baking dish with some of the butter or margarine. Arrange half of the filo sheets in the bottom of the dish to cover evenly and extend about 2.5cm/1in up the sides. Brush with butter.

5 Ladle in the spinach and cheese filling. Cover with the remaining filo pastry, tucking under the edge neatly.

6 Brush the top with the remaining butter. Score the top with diamond shapes using a sharp knife.

7 Bake for about 30 minutes, or until the pastry is golden brown. Cut into squares and serve hot.

Serves 8

1350g/3lb/12 cups fresh spinach, coarse stems removed
30ml/2 tbsp olive oil
1 medium onion, finely chopped
30ml/2 tbsp chopped fresh oregano or 5ml/1 tsp dried oregano
4 eggs
225g/8oz/2 cups creamed low fat cottage cheese
90ml/6 tbsp freshly grated Parmesan cheese
grated nutmeg
60ml/4 tbsp butter or margarine, melted
12 sheets filo pastry
salt and freshly ground black pepper

NUTRITION NOTES
Per portion

Energy	299Kcals/1244kJ
Fat	16.4g
Saturated Fat	4.4g
Cholesterol	105mg
Fibre	3.8g

Celeriac Gratin

Although celeriac has a rather unattractive appearance with its hard, knobbly skin, it is a vegetable that has a very delicious sweet and nutty flavour. This is accentuated in this dish by the addition of the sweet yet nutty Emmenthal cheese.

Serves 4

450g/1lb/3 cups celeriac
juice of ½ lemon
25g/1oz/6 tbsp butter or margarine
1 small onion, finely chopped
30ml/2 tbsp plain flour
300ml/½ pint/1¼ cups skimmed milk
25g/1oz/¼ cup Emmenthal cheese, grated
15ml/1 tbsp capers
salt and cayenne pepper

NUTRITION NOTES

Per portion
Energy	148Kcals/616kJ
Fat	7.7g
Saturated Fat	2.2g
Cholesterol	8mg
Fibre	4.7g

1 Preheat the oven to 190°C/375°F/ Gas 5. Peel the celeriac and cut into 5mm/¼in slices, immediately plunging them into a saucepan of cold water acidulated with the lemon juice.

2 Bring the water to the boil and simmer the celeriac for 10–12 minutes until just tender. Drain and arrange the celeriac in a shallow oven-proof dish.

3 Melt the butter in a small saucepan and fry the onion over a gentle heat until soft but not browned. Stir in the flour, cook for 1 minute, then slowly stir in the milk to make a smooth sauce. Stir in the cheese, capers and seasoning to taste, then pour over the celeriac. Cook in the oven for 15–20 minutes, or until the top is golden brown.

Cook's Tip

For a less strongly flavoured dish, alternate the layers of celeriac with potato. Slice the potato, cook until almost tender, then drain well before assembling the dish.

Baked Leeks with Cheese and Yogurt Topping

Like all vegetables, the fresher leeks are, the better their flavour, and the freshest leeks available should be used for this dish. Small, young leeks are around at the beginning of the season.

1 Preheat the oven to 180°C/350°F/ Gas 4 and butter a shallow ovenproof dish. Trim the leeks, cut a slit from top to bottom and rinse well under cold water.

2 Place the leeks in a saucepan of water, bring to the boil and simmer gently for 6–8 minutes until just tender. Remove and drain well using a slotted spoon, and arrange in the prepared dish.

3 Beat the eggs with the goat's cheese, yogurt and half the Parmesan cheese, and season well with salt and pepper.

4 Pour the cheese and yogurt mixture over the leeks. Mix the breadcrumbs and remaining Parmesan cheese together and sprinkle over the sauce. Bake in the oven for 30–40 minutes, or until the top is crisp and golden brown.

Serves 4
8 small leeks
2 small eggs or 1 large one, beaten
150g/5oz/⅔ cup fresh goat's cheese
85ml/3fl oz/⅓ cup low fat yogurt
50g/2oz/⅓ cup Parmesan cheese, grated
25g/1oz/⅓ cup fresh white or brown breadcrumbs
salt and freshly ground black pepper

NUTRITION NOTES
Per portion

Energy	259Kcals/1082kJ
Fat	15.5g
Saturated Fat	8.2g
Cholesterol	136mg
Fibre	3.8g

Carrot and Coriander Soufflés

Use tender young carrots for this light-as-air dish.

Serves 4
450g/1lb/6-8 carrots
30ml/2 tbsp chopped fresh coriander
4 eggs, separated
salt and freshly ground black pepper

Cook's Tip
Fresh coriander tastes wonderful and it's well worth growing your own coriander plant in a window box to ensure a regular supply. Coriander is also available freeze-dried in some supermarkets – although less impressive than the fresh variety, it is a better alternative than dried herbs.

NUTRITION NOTES
Per portion
Energy	115Kcals/481kJ
Fat	5.8g
Saturated Fat	1.55g
Cholesterol	192.5mg
Fibre	2.7g

1 Peel the carrots.

2 Cook in boiling salted water for 20 minutes or until tender. Drain, and process until smooth in a food processor.

3 Preheat the oven to 200°C/400°F/ Gas 6. Season the pureéd carrots well, and stir in the chopped coriander.

4 Fold the egg yolks into the carrot mixture.

5 In a separate bowl, whisk the egg whites until stiff.

6 Fold the egg whites into the carrot mixture and pour into four greased ramekins. Bake for about 20 minutes or until risen and golden. Serve immediately.

Herb Popovers

Popovers are a muffin-size bread with a crisp brown crust and a delicious moist centre.

Makes 12

3 eggs
250ml/8fl oz/1 cup skimmed milk
30ml/2 tbsp butter, melted
75g/3oz/¾ cup plain flour
0.75ml/⅛ tsp salt
1 small sprig each mixed fresh herbs,
such as chives, tarragon, dill and parsley

NUTRITION NOTES

Per portion
Energy	75Kcals/316kJ
Fat	3.5g
Saturated Fat	0.8g
Cholesterol	49mg
Fibre	0.3g

1 Preheat the oven to 220°C/425°F/ Gas 7. Grease twelve small ramekins or popover cups.

2 With an electric mixer, beat the eggs until blended. Beat in the milk and melted butter.

3 Sift together the flour and salt, then beat into the egg mixture to combine thoroughly.

4 Strip the herb leaves from the stems and chop finely. Mix together and measure out 15ml/2 tbsp. Stir the herbs into the batter.

5 Fill the prepared cups half-full. Bake for 25–30 minutes, or until golden. Do not open the oven door during baking time or the popovers may fall. For drier popovers, pierce each one with a knife after the 30 minutes baking time and bake for 5 minutes more. Serve hot.

Cheese Popovers

Popovers are wonderful when flavoured with a strong cheese such as Parmesan.

1 Preheat the oven to 220°C/425°F/ Gas 7. Grease twelve small ramekins or popover cups.

2 With an electric mixer, beat the eggs until blended. Beat in the milk and melted butter.

3 Sift together the flour, salt and paprika, then beat into the egg mixture. Add the cheese and stir.

4 Fill the prepared cups half-full and bake for 25–30 minutes, or until golden. Do not open the oven door during baking or the popovers may fall. For drier popovers, pierce each one with a knife after the 30 minutes baking time and bake for 5 minutes more. Serve hot.

Variation
To make Yorkshire Pudding Popovers as an accompaniment for roast beef, omit the cheese and use 4–6 table-spoons of the pan drippings to replace the butter. Put them into the oven in time to serve warm with the beef.

Makes 12

3 eggs
250ml/8fl oz/1 cup skimmed milk
30ml/2 tbsp butter, melted
75g/3oz/¾ cup plain flour
1.5ml/¼ tsp salt
1.5ml/¼ tsp paprika
90ml/6 tbsp freshly grated
Parmesan cheese

NUTRITION NOTES
Per portion

Energy	92Kcals/387kJ
Fat	4.8g
Saturated Fat	1.6g
Cholesterol	52mg
Fibre	0.3g

Pumpkin and Ham Frittata

A frittata is an Italian version of the Spanish tortilla, a substantial omelette made from eggs and vegetables. Although frittatas are sometimes eaten cold, this one tastes better warm or hot, served with crusty bread.

Serves 4
30ml/2 tbsp sunflower oil
1 large onion, chopped
450g/1lb/3 cups pumpkin, chopped into bite-size pieces
200ml/7fl oz/scant 1 cup chicken stock
115g/4oz/⅔ cup smoked ham, chopped
6 eggs
10ml/2 tsp chopped fresh marjoram
salt and freshly ground black pepper

NUTRITION NOTES
Per portion

Energy	231Kcals/962kJ
Fat	15.5g
Saturated Fat	3.5g
Cholesterol	308mg
Fibre	1.8g

1 Preheat the oven to 190°C/375°F/ Gas 5 and oil a large shallow oven-proof dish. Heat the oil in a large frying pan and fry the onion for 3–4 minutes until softened.

2 Add the pumpkin and fry over a brisk heat for 3–4 minutes, stirring frequently. Stir in the stock, cover and simmer over a gentle heat for 5–6 minutes until the pumpkin is slightly tender. Add the ham.

3 Pour the mixture into the prepared dish. Beat the eggs with the marjoram and a little seasoning. Pour into the dish and then bake for 20–25 minutes until the frittata is firm and lightly golden.

Wholemeal Herb Triangles

Stuffed with cooked chicken and salad, these make a good lunchtime snack and are also an ideal accompaniment to a bowl of steaming soup.

1 Preheat the oven to 200°C/400°F/ Gas 6. Lightly flour a baking sheet. Put the wholemeal flour in a mixing bowl. Sift in the remaining dry ingredients, including the chilli powder, then rub in the soft margarine.

3 Carefully cut the dough round into eight wedges, separate them slightly and bake for 15–20 minutes. Transfer to a wire rack to cool. Serve warm or cold.

Makes 8

225g/8oz/2 cups wholemeal flour
115g/4oz/1 cup strong plain flour
5ml/1 tsp salt
2.5ml/½ tsp bicarbonate of soda
5ml/1 tsp cream of tartar
2.5ml/½ tsp chilli powder
50g/2oz/¼ cup soft margarine
60ml/4 tbsp chopped mixed fresh herbs
250ml/8fl oz/1 cup skimmed milk
15ml/1 tbsp sesame seeds

NUTRITION NOTES
Per portion
Energy	222Kcals/932kJ
Fat	7.22g
Saturated Fat	1.25g
Cholesterol	1.06mg
Fibre	3.54g

2 Add the herbs and milk and mix quickly to a soft dough. Turn on to a lightly floured surface. Knead only very briefly or the dough will become tough. Roll out to a 23cm/9in round and place on the prepared baking sheet. Brush lightly with water and sprinkle evenly with the sesame seeds.

Cook's Tip
To make Sun-dried Tomato Triangles, replace the mixed fresh herbs with 30ml/2 tbsp drained chopped sun-dried tomatoes in oil and add 15ml/1 tbsp each mild paprika, chopped fresh parsley and chopped fresh marjoram.

Curry Crackers

These spicy, crisp little biscuits are very low in fat and are ideal for serving with drinks.

Makes 12
50g/2oz/½ cup plain flour
1.5ml/¼ tsp salt
5ml/1 tsp curry powder
1.5ml/¼ tsp chilli powder
15ml/1 tbsp chopped fresh coriander
30ml/2 tbsp water

NUTRITION NOTES

Per portion
Energy	15Kcals/65kJ
Fat	0.11g
Saturated Fat	0.01g
Cholesterol	0
Fibre	0.21g

1 Preheat the oven to 180°C/350°F/ Gas 4. Sift the flour and salt into a mixing bowl, then add the curry powder and chilli powder. Make a well in the centre and add the chopped fresh coriander and water. Gradually incorporate the flour and mix to a firm dough.

2 Turn on to a lightly floured surface, knead until smooth, then leave to rest for 5 minutes.

3 Cut the dough into twelve pieces and knead into small balls. Roll each ball out very thinly to a 10cm/4in round.

4 Arrange the rounds on two ungreased baking sheets, then bake for 15 minutes, turning over once during cooking. Cool on a wire rack.

Variation

Omit the curry and chilli powders and add 15ml/1 tbsp caraway, fennel or mustard seeds.

Oatmeal Tartlets with Minted Hummus

Serve these wholesome little tartlets with a crisp salad of cos lettuce.

1 Preheat the oven to 160°C/325°F/ Gas 3. Mix together the oatmeal, bicarbonate of soda and salt in a large bowl. Rub in the butter until the mixture resembles fine crumbs. Stir in the egg yolk and add the milk if the mixture seems too dry.

3 Purée the chick-peas, the juice of one lemon, the fromage blanc and tahini in a food processor until smooth. Spoon into a bowl and season with black pepper and more lemon juice to taste. Stir in the chopped mint. Divide between the tartlet moulds, sprinkle with pumpkin seeds and dust with paprika.

Serves 6

225g/8oz/1⅔ cups medium oatmeal
2.5ml/½ tsp bicarbonate of soda
5ml/1 tsp salt
25g/1oz/2 tbsp butter
1 egg yolk
30ml/2 tbsp skimmed milk
400g/14oz/2 cups canned chick-peas, rinsed and drained
juice of 1–2 lemons
350g/12oz/1½ cups low fat fromage blanc
60ml/4 tbsp tahini
45ml/3 tbsp chopped fresh mint
25g/1oz/2 tbsp pumpkin seeds
freshly ground black pepper
paprika, for dusting

NUTRITION NOTES

Per portion

Energy	365Kcals/1532kJ
Fat	16.8g
Saturated Fat	2.9g
Cholesterol	35mg
Fibre	5.4g

2 Press into 6 x 9cm/3½in tartlet tins. Bake for 25–30 minutes. Allow to cool.

Ham and Tomato Scones

These scones make an ideal accompaniment for soup. Choose a strongly flavoured ham, trimmed of fat, and chop it fairly finely, so that a little goes a long way. Use wholemeal flour or a mixture of wholemeal and white flour for extra flavour.

Serves 12

225g/8oz/2 cups self-raising flour
5ml/1 tsp dry mustard
5ml/1 tsp paprika, plus extra
for sprinkling
2.5ml/½ tsp salt
25g/1oz/2 tbsp soft margarine
15ml/1 tbsp snipped fresh basil
50g/2oz/1 cup drained sun-dried
tomatoes in oil, chopped
50g/2oz/⅓ cup cooked ham, chopped
90–120ml/3–4fl oz/6 tbsp–½ cup
skimmed milk, plus extra
for brushing

NUTRITION NOTES

Per portion
Energy	113Kcals/474kJ
Fat	4.23g
Saturated Fat	0.65g
Cholesterol	2.98mg
Fibre	0.65g

1 Preheat the oven to 200°C/400°F/ Gas 6. Flour a large baking sheet. Sift the flour, mustard, paprika and salt into a bowl. Rub in the margarine until the mixture resembles crumbs.

Cook's Tip
To cut calories and fat, choose dry-packed sun-dried tomatoes and soak them in warm water.

2 Stir in the basil, sun-dried tomatoes and ham, and mix lightly. Pour in enough milk to mix to a soft dough.

3 Turn the dough out on to a lightly floured surface, knead briefly and roll out to a 20 x 15cm/8 x 6in rectangle. Cut into 5cm/2in squares and arrange on the baking sheet.

4 Brush lightly with milk, sprinkle with paprika and bake for about 12–15 minutes. Transfer to a wire rack to cool.

Cheese and Marjoram Scones

A great success for a hearty tea. With savoury toppings, these scones can make a good basis for a light lunch, served with a crunchy, green salad.

1 Gently sift the two kinds of flour into a bowl and add the salt. Cut the butter into small pieces, and rub these into the flour until it resembles fine crumbs.

2 Add the mustard, marjoram and grated cheese, and mix in sufficient milk to make a soft dough. Knead the dough lightly.

3 Preheat the oven to 220°C/425°F/ Gas 7. Roll out the dough on a floured surface to 2cm/¾in thickness and cut it out with a 5cm/2in square cutter. Grease several baking trays with sunflower oil, and place the scones on the trays. Brush the scones with milk and sprinkle the pecans or walnuts over the top. Bake for 12 minutes. Serve warm.

Serves 18

115g/4oz/1 cup wholemeal flour
115g/4oz/1 cup self-raising flour
pinch of salt
40g/1½oz/scant 3 tbsp butter
1.5ml/¼ tsp dry mustard
10ml/2 tsp dried marjoram
50–75g/2–3oz/½–⅔ cup finely grated Cheddar cheese
120ml/4fl oz/½ cup skimmed milk, or as required
5ml/1 tsp sunflower oil
50g/2oz/⅓ cup pecan nuts or walnuts, chopped

NUTRITION NOTES

Per portion
Energy	90Kcals/376kJ
Fat	4.4g
Saturated Fat	0.6g
Cholesterol	1mg
Fibre	0.5g

Oatcakes

Try serving these oatcakes with reduced-fat hard cheeses. They are delicious topped with thick honey for breakfast.

Serves 8

175g/6oz/1¼ cups medium oatmeal, plus extra for sprinkling
2.5ml/½ tsp salt
pinch of bicarbonate of soda
15g/½oz/1 tbsp butter
75ml/5 tbsp water

NUTRITION NOTES

Per portion

Energy	102Kcals/427kJ
Fat	3.43g
Saturated Fat	0.66g
Cholesterol	0.13mg
Fibre	1.49g

1 Preheat the oven to 150°C/300°F/ Gas 2. Mix the oatmeal with the salt and bicarbonate of soda in a bowl.

2 Melt the butter with the water in a small saucepan. Bring to the boil, then add to the oatmeal mixture and mix to a moist dough.

3 Turn the dough on to a surface sprinkled with oatmeal and knead to a smooth ball. Turn a large baking sheet upside down, grease it, sprinkle it lightly with oatmeal and place the ball of dough on top. Sprinkle the dough with oatmeal, then roll out to a 25cm/10in round.

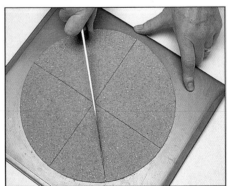

4 Cut the round into eight sections, ease them apart slightly and bake for about 50–60 minutes until crisp. Leave to cool on the baking sheet, then remove the oatcakes with a palette knife.

Dill and Potato Cakes

Potato cakes are quite scrumptious and should be more widely made. Try this splendid combination and you are sure to be converted.

1 Preheat the oven to 230°C/450°F/ Gas 8. Sift the flour into a bowl and add the butter, salt and dill. Mix in the mashed potato and enough milk to make a soft, pliable dough.

2 Roll out the dough on a well-floured surface until it is fairly thin.

3 Cut into neat rounds with a 7.5cm/ 3in cutter.

4 Grease a baking sheet, place the cakes on it, and bake for 20–25 minutes until risen and golden.

Serves 10

225g/8oz/2 cups self-raising flour
45ml/3 tbsp butter, softened
pinch of salt
15ml/1 tbsp finely chopped fresh dill
175g/6oz/scant 1 cup mashed potato, freshly made
30–45ml/2–3 tbsp milk, as required

NUTRITION NOTES
Per portion

Energy	121Kcals/510kJ
Fat	4g
Saturated Fat	0.8g
Cholesterol	0
Fibre	0.9g

Chives and Potato Scones

These little scones should be fairly thin, soft in the middle and crisp on the outside. They're extremely quick to make, so serve them for breakfast or lunch.

Serves 20
450g/1lb/2 large potatoes
115g/4oz/1 cup plain flour, sifted
30ml/2 tbsp olive oil
30ml/2 tbsp snipped chives
salt and freshly ground black pepper
low fat spread, for topping (optional)

NUTRITION NOTES
Per portion
Energy	50 Kcals/211kJ
Fat	1.24g
Saturated Fat	0.17g
Cholesterol	0
Fibre	0.54g

1 Cook the potatoes in a saucepan of boiling salted water for 20 minutes, then drain thoroughly. Return the potatoes to the clean pan and mash them. Preheat a griddle or heavy-based frying pan over a low heat.

2 Add the flour, olive oil and snipped chives with a little salt and pepper to the hot mashed potatoes in the pan. Mix to a soft dough.

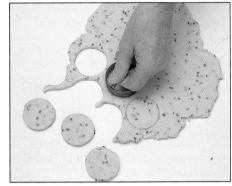

3 Roll out the dough on a well-floured surface to a thickness of 5mm/¼in and stamp out rounds with a 5cm/2in pastry cutter.

4 Cook the scones, in batches, on the hot griddle or frying pan for about 10 minutes until they are golden brown on both sides. Keep the heat low. Top with a little low fat spread, if you like, and serve immediately.

Cheese and Chives Scones

Try serving these savoury scones instead of bread rolls.

1 Preheat the oven to 200°C/400°F/ Gas 6. Sift the flours and salt into a mixing bowl, adding any bran left over from the flour in the sieve.

2 Crumble the feta cheese and rub into the dry ingredients. Stir in the chives, then add the milk and mix to a soft dough.

3 Turn out on to a floured surface and knead lightly until smooth. Roll out to 2cm/¾in thick and stamp out nine scones with a 6cm/2½in biscuit cutter.

4 Transfer the scones to a non-stick baking sheet. Brush with skimmed milk, then sprinkle over the cayenne pepper. Bake in the oven for 15 minutes, or until golden.

Makes 9

115g/4oz/1 cup self-raising flour
150g/5oz/1¼ cup self-raising wholemeal flour
2.5ml/½ tsp salt
75g/3oz/⅓ cup feta cheese
15ml/1 tbsp snipped fresh chives
150ml/¼ pint/⅔ cup skimmed milk, plus extra for glazing
1.5ml/¼ tsp cayenne pepper

NUTRITION NOTES

Per portion

Energy	121Kcals/507kJ
Fat	2.24g
Saturated Fat	1.13g
Cholesterol	0
Fibre	1.92g

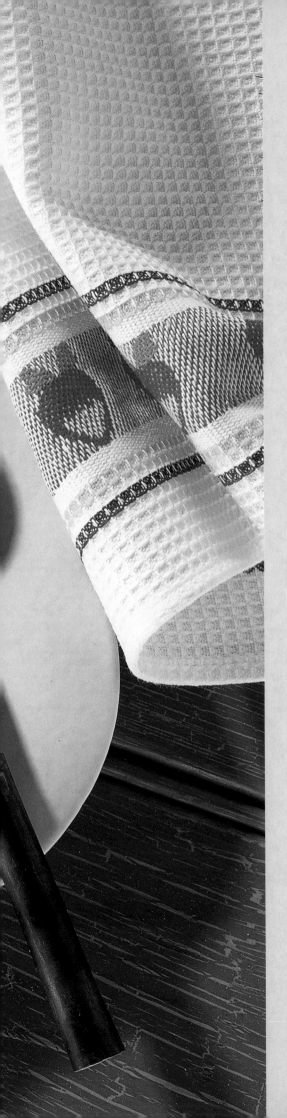

Desserts and Hot Bakes

Everyone will adore
deliciously light
puddings. Serve a fruity
confection to finish a
family meal, or an
elaborate dessert for
a special occasion.

Chestnut and Orange Roulade

This moist cake is ideal to serve as a dessert.

Serves 8

3 eggs, separated
115g/4oz/½ cup caster sugar
225g/8oz/1 cup canned unsweetened
chestnut purée
grated rind and juice of 1 orange
icing sugar, for dusting

For the filling

225g/8oz/1 cup low fat soft cheese
15ml/1 tbsp clear honey
1 orange

Cook's Tip

Do not whisk the egg whites too
stiffly, or it will be difficult to fold
them into the mixture and they
will form lumps in the roulade.

NUTRITION NOTES

Per portion

Energy	185Kcals/775kJ
Fat	4.01g
Saturated Fat	1.47g
Cholesterol	76.25mg
Fibre	1.4g

1 Preheat the oven to 180°C/350°/Gas 4.
Grease a 30 x 20cm/12 x 8in Swiss
roll tin and line with non-stick baking
paper. Whisk the egg yolks and sugar in a
bowl until thick and creamy.

2 Put the chestnut purée in a separate
bowl. Whisk in the orange rind and
juice, then whisk the flavoured chestnut
purée into the egg mixture.

3 Whisk the egg whites in a grease-
free bowl until fairly stiff. Using a
metal spoon, stir a generous spoonful of
the whites into the chestnut mixture to
lighten it, then fold in the rest. Spoon
into the prepared tin and bake for
30 minutes until firm. Cool for 5 minutes,
then cover with a clean damp tea towel
until completely cold.

4 Meanwhile, make the filling. Put the
soft cheese in a bowl with the honey.
Finely grate the orange rind and add to
the bowl. Peel away all the pith from the
orange, cut the fruit into segments, chop
roughly and set aside. Add any juice to
the cheese mixture, then beat until it is
smooth. Mix in the chopped orange.

5 Dust a sheet of greaseproof paper
thickly with icing sugar. Carefully turn
the roulade out on to the paper, then peel
off the lining paper. Spread the filling
over the roulade and roll up like a Swiss
roll. Transfer to a plate and dust with
some more icing sugar.

Chocolate, Date and Walnut Pudding

Proper puddings are not totally taboo when you're cutting calories or fat – this one stays
within the rules! Serve hot, with yogurt or skimmed-milk custard.

Serves 4

25g/1oz/4 tbsp chopped walnuts
25g/1oz/2 tbsp chopped dates
2 eggs
5ml/1 tsp vanilla essence
30ml/2 tbsp golden caster sugar
45ml/3 tbsp plain wholemeal flour
15ml/1 tbsp cocoa powder
30ml/2 tbsp skimmed milk

NUTRITION NOTES

Per portion
Energy   169Kcals/708kJ
Fat   8.1g
Saturated Fat   1.7g
Cholesterol   96mg
Fibre   1.8g

1 Preheat the oven to 180°C/350°F/
Gas 4. Grease a 1.2 litre/2 pint/5 cup
pudding basin and place a small circle of
greaseproof or non-stick baking paper
in the base. Spoon in the walnuts
and dates.

2 Separate the eggs and place the
yolks in a bowl, with the vanilla
essence and sugar. Place the bowl over
a pan of hot water and whisk until the
mixture is thick and pale.

3 Sift the flour and cocoa into the
mixture and fold them in with a metal
spoon. Stir in the milk, to soften the
mixture slightly. Whisk the egg whites
until they hold soft peaks and fold
them in.

4 Spoon the mixture into the basin and
bake for 40–45 minutes, or until the
pudding is well risen and firm to the
touch. Run a knife around the pudding to
loosen it from the basin, and then turn it
out and serve straight away.

Meringues

This is a basic meringue recipe. These light and airy mouthfuls are excellent served with low fat cream.

1 Preheat the oven to 110°C/225°F/ Gas ¼. Grease and flour two large baking sheets.

2 With an electric mixer, beat the egg whites and salt in a very clean metal bowl on low speed. When they start to form soft peaks, add half the sugar and continue beating until the mixture holds stiff peaks.

5 Bake for 2 hours. Turn off the oven. Loosen the meringues, invert, and set in another place on the sheets to prevent sticking. Leave in the oven as it cools. Serve sandwiched with low fat cream, if desired.

Makes 24

4 egg whites
0.75ml/⅛ tsp salt
225g/8oz/1¼ cups caster sugar
2.5ml/½ tsp vanilla or almond essence (optional)
225g/8fl oz/1 cup low fat cream (optional)

NUTRITION NOTES

Per portion

Energy	43Kcals/184kJ
Fat	0
Saturated Fat	0
Cholesterol	0
Fibre	0

3 With a large metal spoon, fold in the remaining sugar and vanilla or almond essence, if using.

4 Pipe the meringue mixture or gently spoon it on to the prepared sheet.

Snowballs

A variation on the basic meringue recipe, these snowballs are made with cornflour.
They make an excellent accompaniment to ice cream.

Makes about 20
2 egg whites
115g/4oz/½ cup caster sugar
15ml/1 tbsp cornflour, sifted
5ml/1 tsp white wine vinegar
1.5ml/¼ tsp vanilla essence

NUTRITION NOTES
Per portion

Energy	29Kcal/124kJ
Fat	0.01
Saturated Fat	0
Cholesterol	0
Fibre	0

1 Preheat the oven to 150°C/300°F/ Gas 2. Line two baking sheets with non-stick baking paper. Whisk the egg whites in a large grease-free bowl until very stiff, using an electric whisk.

2 Add the sugar, whisking until the meringue is very stiff. Whisk in the cornflour, vinegar and vanilla essence.

3 Drop teaspoonfuls of the mixture on to the baking sheets, shaping them into mounds, and bake for 30 minutes until crisp.

4 Remove from the oven and leave to cool on the baking sheet. When the snowballs are cold, remove them from the baking paper with a palette knife.

Muscovado Meringues

These light brown meringues are extremely low in fat and are delicious served on their own or sandwiched together with a fresh fruit soft cheese filling.

1 Preheat the oven to 160°C/325°F/ Gas 3. Line two baking sheets with non-stick baking paper. Press the sugar through a metal sieve into a bowl.

4 Sprinkle the meringues with the chopped walnuts. Bake for 30 minutes. Cool for 5 minutes on the baking sheets, then leave on a wire rack.

Makes about 20

115g/4oz/¾ cup light muscovado sugar
2 egg whites
5ml/1 tsp finely chopped walnuts

NUTRITION NOTES

Per portion

Energy	197Kcals/826kJ
Fat	6.8g
Saturated Fat	1.4g
Cholesterol	25mg
Fibre	0.7g

2 Whisk the egg whites in a clean, dry bowl, until very stiff and dry, then whisk in the sugar, about 15ml/1 tbsp at a time, until the meringue is very thick and glossy.

3 Spoon small mounds of the mixture on to the prepared baking sheets.

Raspberry Vacherin

Meringue rounds filled with orange-flavoured fromage frais and fresh raspberries makes a perfect dinner party dessert.

Serves 6
3 egg whites
175g/6oz/¾ cup caster sugar
5ml/1 tsp chopped almonds
icing sugar, for dusting
raspberry leaves, to
decorate (optional)

For the filling
175g/6oz/¾ cup low fat soft cheese
15–30ml/1–2 tbsp clear honey
15ml/1 tbsp Cointreau
120ml/4 fl oz/½ cup low fat
fromage frais
225g/8oz/1¼ cup raspberries

Cook's Tip
When making the meringue, whisk the egg whites until they are so stiff that you can turn the bowl upside down without them falling out.

NUTRITION NOTES
Per portion

Energy	248Kcals/1041kJ
Fat	2.22g
Saturated Fat	0.82g
Cholesterol	4mg
Fibre	1.06g

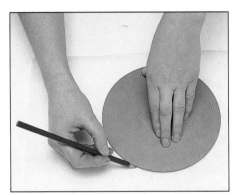

1 Preheat the oven to 140°C/275°F/ Gas 1. Draw a 20cm/8in circle on two pieces of non-stick baking paper. Turn the paper over so the marking is on the underside and use it to line two heavy baking sheets.

2 Whisk the egg whites in a grease-free bowl until very stiff, then gradually whisk in the caster sugar to make a stiff meringue mixture.

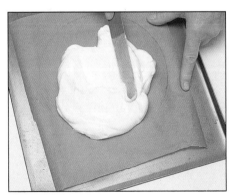

3 Spoon the mixture on to the circles on the prepared baking sheets, spreading the meringue evenly to the edges. Sprinkle one meringue round with the chopped almonds.

4 Bake for 1½–2 hours, then carefully lift the meringue rounds off the baking sheets, peel away the paper and cool on a wire rack.

5 To make the filling, cream the soft cheese with the honey and liqueur in a bowl. Fold in the fromage frais and raspberries, reserving three of the best for decoration.

6 Place the plain meringue round on a board, spread with the filling and top with the nut-covered round. Dust with icing sugar, transfer to a serving plate and decorate with the reserved raspberries, and a sprig of raspberry leaves, if liked.

Toasted Oat Meringues

The oats add an unusual flavour and texture to this interesting dessert.

Makes 12

110g/4oz/¾ cup old-fashioned oats
2 egg whites
0.75ml/⅛ tsp salt
7.5ml/1½ tsp cornstarch
175g/6oz/¾ cup caster sugar

NUTRITION NOTES

Per portion

Energy	98Kcals/416kJ
Fat	0.8g
Saturated Fat	0.2g
Cholesterol	0
Fibre	0.6g

1 Preheat the oven to 140°C/275°F/ Gas 1. Spread the oats on a baking sheet and toast in the oven until golden, for about 10 minutes. Remove the oats and lower the heat to 120°C/ 250°F/ Gas ½. Grease and flour a baking sheet.

Variation

Add 2.5ml/½ tsp ground cinnamon with the oats, and fold in gently.

2 With an electric mixer, beat the egg whites and salt until they start to form soft peaks.

3 Sift over the cornstarch and continue beating until the whites hold stiff peaks. Add half the sugar and whisk until glossy.

4 Add the remaining sugar and fold in, then fold in the toasted oats.

5 Gently spoon mounds of the mixture on to the prepared sheet and bake for 2 hours.

6 When done, turn off the oven. Lift the meringues from the tray, turn over, and set in another place on the sheet to prevent sticking. Leave in the oven as it cools down.

Feather-light Peach Pudding

On chilly days, try this hot fruit pudding with its tantalizing sponge topping.

1 Preheat the oven to 180°C/350°F/
Gas 4. Drain the peaches and put into
a 1 litre/1¾ pint/4 cup pie dish with
30ml/2 tbsp of the juice.

2 Put all the remaining ingredients,
except the icing sugar into a mixing
bowl. Beat for 3–4 minutes, until
thoroughly combined.

3 Spoon the sponge mixture over the
peaches and level the top evenly.
Cook in the oven for 35–40 minutes, or
until springy to the touch.

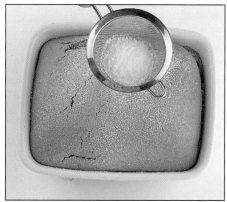

4 Lightly dust the top with icing sugar
before serving hot with the custard.

Cook's Tip

For a simple sauce, blend 5ml/1 tsp
arrowroot with 15ml/1 tbsp peach
juice in a small saucepan. Stir in the
remaining peach juice from the can
and bring to the boil. Simmer for
1 minute until thickened and clear.

Serves 4

400g/14oz/3 cups canned peach slices
in natural juice
50g/2oz/4 tbsp low fat spread
40g/1½ oz/¼ cup soft light brown sugar
1 egg, beaten
50g/2oz/½ cup plain wholemeal flour
50g/2oz/½ cup plain flour
5ml/1 tsp baking powder
2.5ml/½ tsp ground cinnamon
60ml/4 tbsp skimmed milk
2.5ml/½ tsp vanilla essence
10ml/2 tsp icing sugar, for dusting
low fat ready-to-serve custard,
to serve

NUTRITION NOTES

Per portion

Energy	255Kcals/1071kJ
Fat	6.78g
Saturated Fat	1.57g
Cholesterol	35mg
Fibre	2.65g

Strawberry Gâteau

It's hard to believe that this delicious gâteau is low in fat, but it's true, so enjoy!

Serves 6

2 eggs
75g/3oz/⅓ cup caster sugar
grated rind of ½ orange
50g/2oz/½ cup plain flour
strawberry leaves, to
decorate (optional)
icing sugar, for dusting

For the filling

275g/10oz/1¼ cups low fat soft cheese
grated rind of ½ orange
30ml/2 tbsp caster sugar
60ml/4 tbsp low fat fromage frais
225g/8oz strawberries, halved
25g/1oz/¼ cup chopped
almonds, toasted

Cook's Tip

Use other soft fruits in season,
such as currants, raspberries,
blackberries or blueberries, or
try a mixture of different berries.

NUTRITION NOTES

Per portion

Energy	213Kcals/893kJ
Fat	6.08g
Saturated Fat	1.84g
Cholesterol	70.22mg
Fibre	1.02g

1 Preheat the oven to 190°C/375°F/
Gas 5. Grease a 30 x 20cm/12 x 8in
Swiss roll tin and line with non-stick
baking paper.

2 In a bowl, whisk the eggs, sugar and
orange rind together with a hand-held
electric whisk until thick and mousse-like
(when the whisk is lifted, a trail should
remain on the surface of the mixture for
at least 15 seconds).

3 Fold in the flour with a metal spoon,
being careful not to knock out any air.
Turn into the prepared tin. Bake for
15–20 minutes, or until the cake springs
back when lightly pressed. Turn the cake
on to a wire rack, remove the lining paper
and leave to cool.

4 Meanwhile make the filling. In a
bowl, mix the soft cheese with the
orange rind, sugar and fromage frais until
smooth. Divide between two bowls.
Chop half the strawberry halves and add
to one bowl of filling.

5 Cut the sponge widthways into three
equal pieces and sandwich them
together with the strawberry filling.
Spread two-thirds of the plain filling over
the sides of the cake and press on the
toasted almonds.

6 Spread the rest of the filling over the
top of the cake and decorate with
strawberry halves, and strawberry leaves
if liked. Dust with icing sugar and transfer
to a serving plate.

Baked Blackberry Cheesecake

This light, low fat cheesecake is best made with wild blackberries, if they're available, but cultivated ones will do; or substitute other soft fruit, such as loganberries, raspberries or blueberries.

Serves 5

175g/6oz/¾ cup low fat cottage cheese
150g/5oz/⅔ cup low fat natural yogurt
15ml/1 tbsp plain wholemeal flour
25g/1oz/2 tbsp golden caster sugar
1 egg
1 egg white
finely grated rind and juice of ½ lemon
200g/7oz/2 cups fresh or frozen and thawed blackberries

Cook's Tip

If you prefer to use canned blackberries, choose those canned in natural juice and drain the fruit well before adding it to the cheesecake mixture. The juice can be served with the cheesecake, but this will increase the total calories.

NUTRITION NOTES

Per portion
Energy	103Kcals/437kJ
Fat	2g
Saturated Fat	0.8g
Cholesterol	41mg
Fibre	1.6g

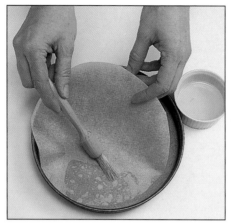

1 Preheat the oven to 180°C/350°F/ Gas 4. Lightly grease and base-line an 18cm/7in sandwich tin.

2 Place the cottage cheese in a food processor and process until smooth. Alternatively, rub it though a sieve, to obtain a smooth mixture.

3 Add the yogurt, flour, sugar, egg and egg white and mix. Add the lemon rind, juice and blackberries, reserving a few for decoration.

4 Tip the mixture into the prepared tin and bake it for 30–35 minutes, or until it is just set. Turn off the oven and leave for a further 30 minutes.

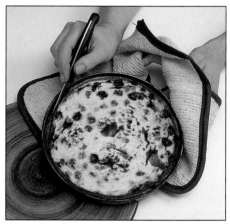

5 Run a knife around the edge of the cheesecake, then turn it out. Remove the lining paper and place the cheese-cake on a warm serving plate.

6 Decorate the cheesecake with the reserved blackberries and serve it warm.

Cherry Clafoutis

When fresh cherries are in season, this makes a deliciously simple dessert for any occasion.
Serve warm with a little fromage frais.

Serves 6

675g/1½lb/3 cups fresh cherries
50g/2oz/½ cup plain flour
pinch of salt
4 eggs, plus 2 egg yolks
115g/4oz/½ cup caster sugar
600ml/1 pint/2½ cups milk
50g/2oz/¼ cup melted butter
caster sugar, for dusting

NUTRITION NOTES

Per portion
Energy	312Kcals/1308kJ
Fat	12.6g
Saturated Fat	2.9g
Cholesterol	198mg
Fibre	1g

1 Preheat the oven to 190°C/375°F/ Gas 5. Lightly butter the base and sides of a shallow ovenproof dish. Stone the cherries and place in the dish.

2 Sift the flour and salt into a bowl. Add the eggs, egg yolks, sugar and a little of the milk and whisk to a smooth batter.

3 Gradually whisk in the rest of the milk and the butter, then strain the batter over the cherries. Bake for 40–50 minutes until golden and just set. Serve warm, dusted with caster sugar, if you like.

Cook's Tip
Use two 425g/15oz cans stoned black cherries, thoroughly drained, if fresh cherries are not available. For a special dessert, add 45ml/3 tbsp kirsch to the batter.

Filo Fruit Baskets

These little baskets are an easy dinner party dessert.

1 Preheat the oven to 180°C/350°F/ Gas 4. Grease six cups of a muffin tin.

2 Stack the filo sheets and cut with a sharp knife or scissors into 24 x 11cm/4½in squares.

3 Lay four squares of pastry in each of the six muffin cups. Press the pastry firmly into the cups, rotating slightly to make star-shaped baskets.

4 Brush the pastry baskets lightly with butter or margarine. Bake for 5–7 minutes, or until the pastry is crisp and golden. Cool on a wire rack.

5 In a bowl, lightly whip the cream until soft peaks form. Gently fold the strawberry preserves and orange liqueur into the cream.

6 Just before serving, spoon a little of the cream mixture into each pastry basket. Top with the fruit. Sprinkle with icing sugar and decorate each basket with a small sprig of mint.

Serves 6

4 large or 8 small sheets filo pastry, thawed if frozen
75ml/5 tbsp butter or margarine, melted
225g/8fl oz/1 cup whipping cream
75g/3oz/¼ cup strawberry preserves
15ml/1 tbsp Cointreau or other orange liqueur
175g/6oz/1 cup seedless red grapes, halved
175g/6oz/1 cup seedless green grapes, halved
175g/6oz/1 cup fresh pineapple cubes
175g/6oz/1 cup raspberries
30ml/2 tbsp icing sugar
6 small sprigs of fresh mint, for garnishing

NUTRITION NOTES

Per portion
Energy	255Kcals/1063kJ
Fat	11g
Saturated Fat	2.2g
Cholesterol	1mg
Fibre	0.9g

Blueberry and Orange Crêpe Baskets

Impress your guests with these pretty, fruit-filled crêpes. When blueberries are out of season, replace them with other soft fruit, such as raspberries.

Serves 6

For the pancakes
150g/5oz/1¼ cups plain flour
pinch of salt
2 egg whites
200ml/7fl oz/⅞ cup skimmed milk
150ml/¼ pint/⅔ cup orange juice

For the filling
4 medium-size oranges
225g/8oz/2 cups blueberries

1 Preheat the oven to 200°C/400°F/ Gas 6. To make the pancakes, sift the flour and salt into a bowl. Make a well in the centre of the flour and add the egg whites, milk and orange juice. Whisk hard, until all the liquid has been incorporated and the batter is smooth and bubbly.

2 Lightly grease a heavy or non-stick pancake pan and heat until it is very hot. Pour in just enough batter to cover the base of the pan, swirling it to cover the pan evenly.

Cook's Tip
Don't fill the pancake baskets until you're ready to serve them, because they will absorb the fruit juice and begin to soften.

3 Cook until the pancake has set and is golden, and then turn it to cook the other side. Remove the pancake to a sheet of absorbent kitchen paper, and then cook the remaining batter, to make 6–8 pancakes.

4 Place six small ovenproof bowls or moulds on a baking sheet and arrange the pancakes over these. Bake the pancakes in the oven for about 10 minutes, until they are crisp and set into the shape of the moulds. Carefully lift the "baskets" off the moulds.

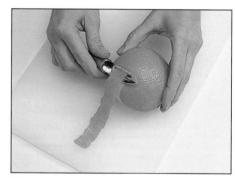

5 For the filling, pare a thin piece of orange rind from one orange and cut it in fine strips. Blanch the strips in boiling water for 30 seconds, rinse in cold water and set aside. Cut all the peel and white pith from all the oranges.

6 Divide the oranges into segments, catching the juice, combine with the blueberries and warm them gently. Spoon the fruit into the baskets and scatter the shreds of rind over the top. Serve with yogurt or light crème fraîche.

NUTRITION NOTES
Per portion

Energy	159Kcals/673kJ
Fat	0.5g
Saturated Fat	0.1g
Cholesterol	1mg
Fibre	3.3g

Filo and Apricot Purses

Filo pastry is very easy to use and is low in fat. Keep a packet in the freezer ready for rustling up a speedy tea-time treat.

Makes 12

115g/4oz/¾ cup ready-to-eat
dried apricots
45ml/3 tbsp apricot compote or
conserve
3 amaretti biscuits, crushed
3 sheets filo pastry
20ml/4 tsp soft margarine, melted
icing sugar, for dusting

NUTRITION NOTES

Per portion	
Energy	58Kcals/245kJ
Fat	1.85g
Saturated Fat	0.4g
Cholesterol	0.12mg
Fibre	0.74g

1 Preheat the oven to 180°C/350°F/ Gas 4. Grease two baking sheets. Chop the apricots, put them in a bowl and stir in the apricot compote. Add the crushed amaretti biscuits and mix well.

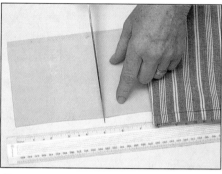

2 Cut the filo pastry into 24 13cm/5in squares, pile the squares on top of each other and cover with a clean tea towel to prevent the pastry from drying out and becoming brittle.

3 Lay one pastry square on a flat surface, brush lightly with melted margarine and lay another square diagonally on top. Brush the top square with melted margarine. Spoon a small mound of apricot mixture in the centre of the pastry, bring up the edges and pinch together in a money-bag shape. Repeat with the remaining filo squares and filling to make 12 purses in all.

4 Arrange the purses on the prepared baking sheets and bake for 5–8 minutes until golden brown. Transfer to a wire rack and dust lightly with icing sugar. Serve warm.

Filo Scrunchies

Quick and easy to make, these pastries are ideal to serve at tea time. Eat them warm
or they will lose their crispness.

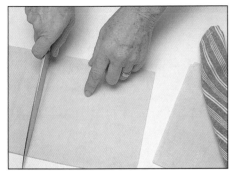

1 Preheat the oven to 190°C/375°F/
Gas 5. Halve the apricots or plums,
remove the stones and slice the fruit. Cut
the filo pastry into twelve 18cm/7in
squares. Pile the squares on top of each
other and cover with a clean tea towel to
prevent the pastry from drying out.

4 Place the scrunchies on a baking
sheet. Bake for 8–10 minutes until
golden brown, then loosen the
scrunchies from the baking sheet with
a palette knife and transfer to a wire
rack. Dust with icing sugar and serve
at once.

Makes 6

5 apricots or plums
4 sheets filo pastry
20ml/4 tsp soft margarine, melted
50g/2oz/⅓ cup demerara sugar
30ml/2 tbsp flaked almonds
icing sugar, for dusting

NUTRITION NOTES
Per portion
Energy	132Kcals/555kJ
Fat	4.19g
Saturated Fat	0.63g
Cholesterol	0
Fibre	0.67g

2 Remove one square of filo and brush
it with melted margarine. Lay a
second filo square on top, then, using
your fingers, mould the pastry into folds.
Make five more scrunchies in the same
way, working quickly so that the pasty
does not dry out.

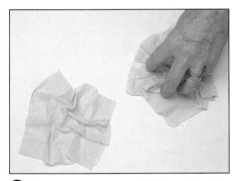

3 Arrange a few slices of fruit in the
folds of each scrunchie, then sprinkle
generously with the demerara sugar and
flaked almonds.

Plum Filo Pockets

These attractive party parcels are high in fibre as well as being a tasty treat.

Serves 4

115g/4oz/½ cup skimmed
milk soft cheese
15ml/1 tbsp light muscovado sugar
2.5ml/½ tsp ground cloves
8 large, firm plums, halved and stoned
8 sheets filo pastry
sunflower oil, for brushing
icing sugar, to sprinkle

NUTRITION NOTES

Per portion

Energy	188Kcals/790kJ
Fat	1.87g
Saturated Fat	0.27g
Cholesterol	0.29mg
Fibre	2.55g

1 Preheat the oven to 220°C/425°F/ Gas 7. Mix together the cheese, sugar and cloves.

2 Sandwich the plum halves back together with a spoonful of the cheese mixture in each plum.

3 Spread out the pastry and cut into 16 pieces, about 23cm/9in square. Brush one lightly with oil and place a second at a diagonal on top. Repeat with the remaining squares.

4 Place a plum on each pastry square, and gather the corners together. Place on a baking sheet. Bake for 15–18 minutes, until golden, then dust with icing sugar.

Apple Couscous Pudding

This unusual mixture makes a delicious family pudding with a rich, fruity flavour, but virtually no fat.

1 Preheat the oven to 200°C/400°F/ Gas 6. Place the apple juice, couscous, sultanas and spice in a pan and bring to the boil, stirring. Cover and simmer for 10–12 minutes, until all the free liquid is absorbed.

3 Arrange the remaining apple slices overlapping on top and sprinkle with demerara sugar. Bake for 25–30 minutes, or until golden brown. Serve hot, with low fat yogurt.

Serves 4

600ml/1 pint/2½ cups apple juice
115g/4oz/⅔ cup couscous
40g/1½oz/¼ cup sultanas
2.5ml/½ tsp mixed spice
1 large Bramley cooking apple, peeled, cored and sliced
30ml/2 tbsp demerara sugar
natural low fat yogurt, to serve

NUTRITION NOTES

Per portion

Energy	194Kcals/815kJ
Fat	0.58g
Saturated Fat	0.09g
Cholesterol	0
Fibre	0.75g

2 Spoon half the couscous mixture into a 1.2 litre/2 pint/5 cup ovenproof dish and top with half the apple slices. Top with the remaining couscous.

Filo Chiffon Pie

Filo pastry is low in fat and very easy to use. Here is an interesting and delicious alternative to rhubarb crumbles and pies that are more traditional.

Serves 3

500g/1¼lb/6 cups pink rhubarb
5ml/1 tsp mixed spice
finely grated rind and juice of 1 orange
15ml/1 tsp granulated sweetener
15g/½oz/1 tbsp butter
3 sheets filo pastry

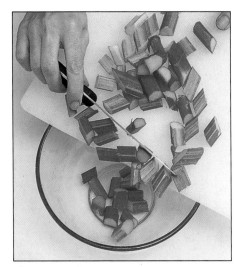

1 Preheat the oven to 200°C/400°F/ Gas 6. Trim the leaves and ends from the rhubarb sticks and chop them in 2.5cm/1in pieces. Place them in a bowl.

3 Melt the butter and brush it over the pastry. Lift the pastry on to the pie dish, butter-side up, and crumple it up to form a chiffon effect, covering the pie completely.

2 Add the mixed spice, orange rind and juice and sweetener and toss well to coat evenly. Tip the rhubarb into a 1 litre/1¾ pint/4 cup pie dish.

4 Place the dish on a baking sheet and bake it for 20 minutes, until golden brown. Reduce the heat to 180°C/350°F/ Gas 4 and bake for a further 10–15 minutes, until the rhubarb is tender. Serve warm.

Cook's Tip

Other fruit such as apples, pear or peaches can be used in this pie – try it with whatever is in season.

NUTRITION NOTES

Per portion

Energy	158Kcals/660kJ
Fat	5.3g
Saturated Fat	1g
Cholesterol	0
Fibre	2.4g

Mango and Amaretti Strudel

Fresh mango and crushed amaretti wrapped in wafer-thin filo pastry make a special treat that is equally delicious made with apricots or plums.

Serves 4
1 large mango
grated rind of 1 lemon
2 amaretti biscuits
25g/1oz/3 tbsp demerara sugar
60ml/4 tbsp wholemeal breadcrumbs
2 sheets filo pastry, each
48 x 28cm/19 x 11in
20g/¾oz/4 tsp soft margarine, melted
15ml/1 tbsp chopped almonds
icing sugar, for dusting

Cook's Tip
The easiest way to prepare a mango is to cut horizontally through the fruit, keeping the knife blade close to the stone. Repeat on the other side of the stone and peel off the skin. Remove the remaining skin and flesh from around the stone.

NUTRITION NOTES
Per portion

Energy	239Kcals/1006kJ
Fat	8.45g
Saturated Fat	4.43g
Cholesterol	17.25mg
Fibre	3.3g

1 Preheat the oven to 190°C/375°F/ Gas 5. Lightly grease a large baking sheet. Halve, stone and peel the mango. Cut the flesh into cubes, then place them in a bowl, and sprinkle with grated lemon rind.

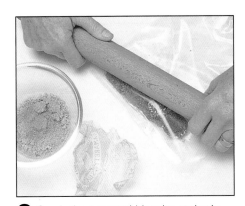

2 Crush the amaretti biscuits and mix them with the demerara sugar and the wholemeal breadcrumbs.

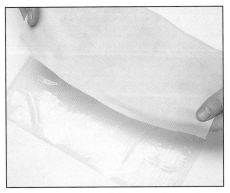

3 Lay one sheet of filo on a flat surface and brush with a quarter of the melted margarine. Top with the second sheet, brush with one-third of the remaining margarine, then fold both sheets over, if necessary, to make a rectangle measuring 28 x 24cm/11 x 9in. Brush with half the remaining margarine.

4 Sprinkle the filo with the amaretti mixture, leaving a 5cm/2in border on each long side. Arrange the mango cubes over the top.

5 Roll up the filo from one of the long sides, Swiss roll-style fashion. Lift the strudel on to the baking sheet with the join underneath. Brush with the remaining melted margarine and sprinkle with the chopped almonds.

6 Bake for 20–25 minutes until golden brown, then transfer to a board. Dust with the icing sugar, slice diagonally and serve warm.

Chunky Apple Bake

This filling, economical family pudding is a good way to use up slightly stale bread – any type of bread will do, but wholemeal is richest in fibre.

Serves 4

450g/1lb/2¼ cups Bramley or other cooking apples
75g/3oz wholemeal bread, without crusts
115g/4oz/½ cup low fat cottage cheese
45ml/3 tbsp light muscovado sugar
200ml/7fl oz/⅞ cup semi-skimmed milk
5ml/1 tsp demerara sugar

Cook's Tip

You may need to adjust the amount of milk used, depending on the dryness of the bread; the more stale the bread, the more milk it will absorb.

NUTRITION NOTES

Per portion

Energy	168Kcals/707kJ
Fat	1g
Saturated Fat	0.4g
Cholesterol	2mg
Fibre	2.9g

1 Preheat the oven to 220°C/425°F/ Gas 7. Peel the apples, cut them into quarters and remove the cores.

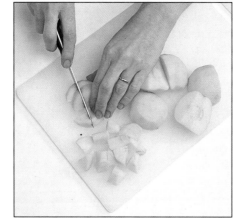

2 Roughly chop the apples into even-size pieces, about 1cm/½in across.

3 Cut the bread into 1cm/½in dice.

4 Toss together the apples, bread, cottage cheese and muscovado sugar in a bowl.

5 Stir in the milk and then tip the mixture into a wide ovenproof dish. Sprinkle with the demerara sugar.

6 Bake for 30–35 minutes, or until golden brown and bubbling. Serve hot.

Baked Apple in Honey and Lemon

A classic mix of flavours in a healthy, traditional family pudding. Serve warm, with skimmed-milk custard.

Serves 4

4 medium-size cooking apples
15ml/1 tbsp clear honey
grated rind and juice of 1 lemon
15ml/1 tbsp low fat spread

NUTRITION NOTES

Per portion

Energy	651Kcals/2703kJ
Fat	1.7g
Saturated Fat	0.4g
Cholesterol	0
Fibre	1.7g

1 Preheat the oven to 180°C/350°F/ Gas 4. Remove the cores from the apples, leaving them whole.

2 With a cannelle or sharp knife, cut lines through the apple skin at intervals and place in an ovenproof dish.

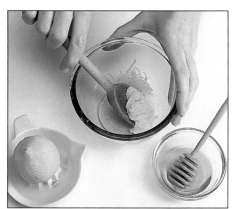

3 Mix together the honey, lemon rind, juice and low fat spread.

4 Spoon the mixture into the apples and cover the dish with foil or a lid. Bake for 40–45 minutes, or until the apples are tender. Serve with skimmed-milk custard.

Strawberry and Apple Crumble

A high fibre, healthier version of the classic apple crumble. Raspberries can be used instead of strawberries, either fresh or frozen. Serve warm, with skimmed-milk custard.

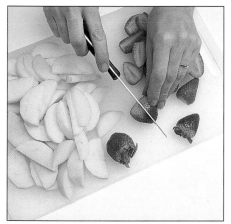

1 Preheat the oven to 180°C/350°F/ Gas 4. Peel, core and slice the apples. Halve the strawberries.

2 Toss together the apples, strawberries, sweetener, cinnamon and orange juice. Tip into a 1.2 litre/2 pint/5 cup oven-proof dish, or four individual dishes.

3 Combine the flour and oats in a bowl and mix in the low fat spread with a fork.

4 Sprinkle the crumble evenly over the fruit. Bake for 40–45 minutes (20–25 minutes for individual dishes), until golden brown and bubbling. Serve warm, with low fat custard or yogurt.

Serves 4
450g/1lb cooking apples
150g/5oz/1¼ cups strawberries, hulled
30ml/2 tbsp granulated sweetener
2.5ml/½ tsp ground cinnamon
30ml/2 tbsp orange juice

For the crumble
45ml/3 tbsp plain wholemeal flour
50g/2oz/⅔ cups porridge oats
25g/1oz/⅛ cup low fat spread

NUTRITION NOTES

Per portion

Energy	182Kcals/769kJ
Fat	4g
Saturated Fat	0.9g
Cholesterol	0
Fibre	3.5g

Mixed Berry Tart

The orange-flavoured pastry of this tart is delicious with the fresh fruits of summer.
Serve this with some extra shreds of orange rind scattered on top.

Serves 8

For the pastry
225g/8oz/2 cups plain flour
115g/4oz/½ cup unsalted butter
finely grated rind of 1 orange, plus
extra to decorate

For the filling
300ml/½ pint/1¼ cups crème fraîche
finely grated rind of 1 lemon
10ml/2 tsp icing sugar
675g/1½lb/6 cups mixed
summer berries

1 To make the pastry, put the flour and butter in a large bowl. Rub in the butter until the mixture resembles breadcrumbs.

2 Add the orange rind and enough cold water to make a soft dough.

3 Roll into a ball and chill for at least 20 minutes. Roll out the pastry on a lightly floured surface.

4 Line a 23cm/9in loose-based flan tin with the pastry. Chill for 30 minutes. Preheat the oven to 200°C/400°F/Gas 6 and place a baking sheet in the oven to heat up. Weight the pastry base with greaseproof paper and baking beans and bake blind on the baking sheet for 15 minutes. Remove the paper and beans and bake the pastry for 10 minutes, until it is golden. Allow to cool.

5 To make the filling, whisk the crème fraîche, lemon rind and sugar together and pour into the pastry case. Top with fruit, sprinkle with orange rind and serve sliced.

NUTRITION NOTES

Per portion

Energy	293Kcals/1223kJ
Fat	17.9g
Saturated Fat	5.9g
Cholesterol	40mg
Fibre	2.4g

Crunchy Gooseberry Crumble

Gooseberries are perfect for traditional family puddings like this one. When they are out of season, other fruits such as apples, plums or rhubarb could be used instead.

Serves 4

500g/1¼lb/5 cups gooseberries
50g/2oz/4 tbsp caster sugar
75g/3oz/1 cup rolled oats
75g/3oz/¾ cups wholemeal flour
60ml/4 tbsp sunflower oil
50g/2oz/4 tbsp demerara sugar
30ml/2 tbsp chopped walnuts
low fat yogurt or custard, to serve

NUTRITION NOTES

Per portion

Energy	422Kcals/1770kJ
Fat	18.5g
Saturated Fat	2.32g
Cholesterol	0
Fibre	5.12g

1 Preheat the oven to 200°C/400°F/ Gas 6. Place the gooseberries in a pan with the caster sugar. Cover the pan and cook over a low heat for 10 minutes, until the gooseberries are just tender. Tip into an ovenproof dish.

2 To make the crumble, place the oats, flour and oil in a bowl, and stir with a fork until evenly mixed.

3 Stir in the demerara sugar and walnuts, then spread evenly over the gooseberries. Bake for 25–30 minutes, or until golden and bubbling. Serve hot with low fat yogurt, or custard made with skimmed milk.

Cook's Tip

The best cooking gooseberries are the early small, firm green ones.

Ginger Upside Down Pudding

A traditional pudding goes down well on a cold winter's day. This one is quite quick to make and looks very impressive.

1 Preheat the oven to 180°C/350°F/ Gas 4. For the topping, brush the base and sides of a 23cm/9in round spring form cake tin with oil. Sprinkle the sugar over the base.

2 Arrange the peaches cut-side down in the tin with a walnut half in each.

3 For the base, sift together the flour, bicarbonate of soda, ginger and cinnamon, then stir in the sugar. Beat together the egg, milk and oil, then mix into the dry ingredients until smooth.

4 Pour the mixture evenly over the peaches and bake for 35–40 minutes, until firm to the touch. Turn out on to a serving plate. Serve hot with low fat yogurt or custard.

Serves 4–6
sunflower oil, for brushing
15ml/1 tbsp soft brown sugar
4 medium peaches, halved and stoned, or canned peach halves
8 walnut halves

For the base
115g/4oz/½ cup wholemeal flour
2.5ml/½ tsp bicarbonate of soda
7.5ml/1½ tsp ground ginger
5ml/1 tsp ground cinnamon
115g/4oz/½ cup molasses sugar
1 egg
120ml/4fl oz/½ cup skimmed milk
50ml/2fl oz/¼ cup sunflower oil

NUTRITION NOTES
Per portion
Energy	432Kcals/1812kJ
Fat	16.54g
Saturated Fat	2.27g
Cholesterol	48.72mg
Fibre	4.79g

Latticed Peaches

An elegant dessert; it certainly doesn't look low in fat, but it really is. Use canned peach halves when fresh peaches are out of season, or if you're short of time.

Serves 6
For the pastry
115g/4oz/1 cup plain flour
45ml/3 tbsp butter or
sunflower margarine
45ml/3 tbsp low fat natural yogurt
30ml/2 tbsp orange juice
skimmed milk, for glaze

For the filling
3 ripe peaches or nectarines
45ml/3 tbsp ground almonds
30ml/2 tbsp low fat natural yogurt
finely grated rind of 1 small orange
1.5ml/¼ tsp natural almond essence

For the sauce
1 ripe peach or nectarine
45ml/3 tbsp orange juice

Cook's Tip

This dessert is best eaten fairly fresh from the oven, as the pastry can toughen slightly if left to stand. So assemble the peaches in their pastry on a baking sheet, chill in the fridge, and bake just before serving.

NUTRITION NOTES

Per portion
Energy	219Kcal/916kJ
Fat	10.8g
Saturated Fat	1.6g
Cholesterol	1mg
Fibre	2.4g

1 For the pastry, sift the flour into a bowl and, using your fingertips, rub in the butter or margarine evenly. Stir in the yogurt and orange juice to bind the mixture into a firm dough.

2 Roll out about half the pastry thinly and use a biscuit cutter to stamp out rounds about 7.5cm/3in in diameter, slightly larger than the circumference of the peaches. Place on a lightly greased baking sheet.

3 Skin the peaches or nectarines, halve and remove the stones. Mix together the almonds, yogurt, orange rind and almond essence. Spoon into the hollows of each peach half and place, cut-side down, on to the pastry rounds.

4 Roll out the remaining pastry thinly and cut into thin strips. Arrange the strips over the peaches to form a lattice, brushing with milk to secure firmly. Trim off the ends neatly.

5 Chill in the fridge for 30 minutes. Preheat the oven to 200°C/ 400°F/ Gas 6. Brush with milk and bake for 15–18 minutes, until golden brown.

6 For the sauce, skin the peach or nectarine and halve it to remove the stone. Place the flesh in a food processor, with the orange juice, and purée it until smooth. Serve the peaches hot, with the peach sauce spooned around.

Hot Plum Batter

Other fruits can be used in place of plums, depending on the season. Canned black cherries are also a convenient storecupboard substitute.

Serves 4

450g/1lb/2½ cups ripe red plums,
quartered and stoned
200ml/7fl oz/⅞ cup skimmed milk
60ml/4 tbsp skimmed milk powder
15ml/1 tbsp light muscovado sugar
5ml/1 tsp vanilla essence
75g/3oz/¾ cup self-raising flour
2 egg whites
icing sugar, to sprinkle

NUTRITION NOTES

Per portion
Energy	195Kcals/816kJ
Fat	0.48g
Saturated Fat	0.12g
Cholesterol	2.8mg
Fibre	2.27g

1 Preheat the oven to 220°C/425°F/ Gas 7. Lightly oil a wide, shallow ovenproof dish and add the plums.

2 Pour the milk, milk powder, sugar, vanilla, flour and egg whites into a food processor. Process until smooth.

3 Pour the batter over the plums. Bake for 25-30 minutes, or until well risen and golden. Sprinkle with icing sugar and serve immediately.

Glazed Apricot Sponge

Puddings can be very high in saturated fat, but this one uses the minimum of oil and no eggs.

1 Preheat the oven to 180°C/350°F/ Gas 4. Lightly oil a 900ml/1½ pint/ 3¾ cup pudding basin. Spoon in the syrup.

3 Mix the flour, breadcrumbs, sugar and cinnamon, then beat in the oil and milk. Spoon into the basin and bake for 50–55 minutes, or until firm and golden. Turn out and serve with the puréed fruit as a sauce.

2 Drain the apricots and reserve the juice. Arrange about eight halves in the basin. Purée the rest of the apricots with the juice and set aside.

Serves 4

10ml/2 tsp golden syrup

411g/14½oz can apricot halves in fruit juice

150g/5oz/1¼ cup self-raising flour

75g/3oz/1½ cups fresh breadcrumbs

90g/3½oz/⅔ cup light muscovado sugar

5ml/1 tsp ground cinnamon

30ml/2 tbsp sunflower oil

175ml/6fl oz/¾ cup skimmed milk

NUTRITION NOTES

Per portion

Energy	364Kcals/1530kJ
Fat	6.47g
Saturated Fat	0.89g
Cholesterol	0.88mg
Fibre	2.37g

Fruity Bread Pudding

A delicious family favourite pudding from grandmother's day, with a lighter healthier touch.

Serves 4

75g/3oz/⅔ cup mixed dried fruit
150ml/¼ pint/⅔ cup apple juice
115g/4oz/2 cups stale brown or white
bread, diced
5ml/1 tsp mixed spice
1 large banana, sliced
150ml/¼ pint/⅔ cup skimmed milk
15ml/1 tbsp demerara sugar
natural low fat yogurt, to serve

NUTRITION NOTES

Per portion
Energy	190Kcals/800kJ
Fat	0.89g
Saturated Fat	0.21g
Cholesterol	0.75mg
Fibre	1.8g

1 Preheat the oven to 200°C/400°F/ Gas 6. Place the dried fruit in a small pan with the apple juice and bring to the boil.

2 Remove the pan from the heat and stir in the bread, spice and banana. Spoon the mixture into a shallow 1.2litre/ 2 pint/5 cup ovenproof dish and pour over the milk.

3 Sprinkle with demerara sugar and bake for 25–30 minutes, until firm and golden brown. Serve hot or cold with natural low fat yogurt.

Cook's Tip

Different types of bread will absorb varying amounts of liquid, so you may need to adjust the amount of milk to allow for this.

Souffléed Orange Semolina

Semolina has a poor reputation as a rather dull, sloppy pudding, but cooked like this you would hardly recognise it.

1 Preheat the oven to 200°C/400°F/ Gas 6. Place the semolina in a non-stick pan with the milk and sugar. Stir over a moderate heat until thickened and smooth. Remove from the heat.

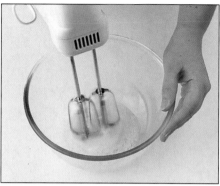

3 Whisk the egg white until stiff but not dry, then fold lightly and evenly into the mixture. Spoon into a 1 litre/ 1¾ pint/4 cup ovenproof dish and bake for 15–20 minutes, until risen and golden brown. Serve immediately.

Serves 4

50g/2oz/¼ cup semolina
600ml/1 pint/2½ cups semi-skimmed milk
30ml/2 tbsp light muscovado sugar
1 large orange
1 egg white

NUTRITION NOTES

Per portion
Energy	158Kcals/665kJ
Fat	2.67g
Saturated Fat	1.54g
Cholesterol	10.5mg
Fibre	0.86g

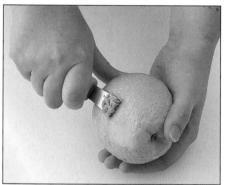

2 Grate a few long shreds of orange rind from the orange and save for decoration. Finely grate the remaining rind. Cut all the peel and white pith from the orange and remove the segments. Stir the fruit into the semolina with the orange rind.

Cook's Tip

When using the rind of citrus fruit, scrub the fruit thoroughly before use, or buy unwaxed fruit.

Souffléed Rice Pudding

The fluffy egg whites in this unusually light rice pudding make the portions seem much more substantial, without adding lots of extra calories or fat.

Serves 4

50g/2oz/¼ cup short-grain rice
45ml/3 tbsp clear honey
750ml/1¼ pints/3¾ cups semi-skimmed milk
1 vanilla pod or 2.5ml/½ tsp vanilla essence
2 egg whites
5ml/1 tsp freshly grated nutmeg

Cook's Tip

If you wish, use skimmed milk instead of semi-skimmed, but take care when it's simmering as with so little fat, it tends to boil over very easily.

NUTRITION NOTES

Per portion
Energy	161Kcals/679kJ
Fat	0.9g
Saturated Fat	0.1g
Cholesterol	4mg
Fibre	0

1 Place the rice, honey and milk in a heavy or non-stick pan and bring the milk to the boil. Add the vanilla pod, if using it.

2 Reduce the heat and put the lid on the pan. Leave to simmer gently for about 1–1¼ hours, stirring occasionally to prevent sticking, until most of the liquid has been absorbed.

3 Remove the vanilla pod, or if using vanilla essence, add this to the rice mixture now. Preheat the oven to 220°C/425°F/Gas 7.

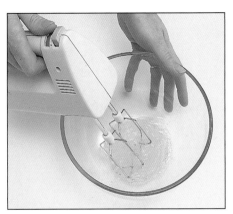

4 Place the egg whites in a clean, dry bowl and whisk them until they hold soft peaks.

5 Using a metal spoon or spatula, fold the egg whites evenly into the rice mixture and tip into a 1 litre/1¾ pint/4 cup ovenproof dish.

6 Sprinkle with grated nutmeg and bake for 15–20 minutes, until the pudding is well-risen and golden brown. Serve hot.

Index

Acknowledgements

The publishers would like to thank the following contributing authors: Catherine Atkinson, Jacqueline Clark, Frances Cleary, Roz Denny, Joanna Farrow, Christine France, Shirley Gill, Carole Handslip, Shezad Husain, Annie Nichols, Maggie Pannell, Katherine Richmond, Anne Sheasby, Liz Trigg and Laura Washburn. The publishers would also like to thank the following photographers: Karl Adamson, Steve Baxter, James Duncan, Michelle Garrett, Amanda Heywood, Don Last and Michael Michaels.